THE
oracle
OF
ORACLE

THE
oracle
OF
ORACLE

the story of volatile
CEO Larry Ellison
and the strategies
behind his company's
phenomenal success

FLORENCE M. STONE

AMACOM AMERICAN MANAGEMENT ASSOCIATION
New York • Atlanta • Brussels • Buenos Aires • Chicago
London • Mexico City • San Francisco • Shanghai • Tokyo
Toronto • Washington, D. C.

This publication is designed to provide accurate and authoritative information in regard to the subject matter covered. It is sold with the understanding that the publisher is not engaged in rendering legal, accounting, or other professional service. If legal advice or other expert assistance is required, the services of a competent professional person should be sought.

Library of Congress Cataloging-in-Publication Data
Stone, Florence M., 1945—
    The Oracle of Oracle : the story of volatile CEO Larry Ellison and the strategies behind his company's phenomenal success / Florence M. Stone.
        p. cm.
    Includes bibliographical references and index.
    ISBN 0-8144-0639-4
    1. Ellison, Larry. 2. Oracle Corporation—History. 3. Computer software industry—United States—History. 4. Businesspeople—United States—Biography.

    HD9696.63.U62 E447 2002
    338.7/610053/0973 21

                                                                    2001055225

Printing number

10 9 8 7 6 5 4 3 2 1

THIS BOOK IS DEDICATED
TO MY MOM.

contents

preface

Over the years as a writer and editor, I have written about numerous CEOs. None of the profiles I have done began with such an ambiguous understanding of the subject—Larry Joseph Ellison—and ended with similar perplexity as the book you hold in your hand. The time it takes to research then write a book did not help, either. As I began this book, the dot-com shakeout had not occurred; as I finish this Preface, we are well past suspicions of an economic downturn and have entered into a true slump, nowhere more evident than in the high-tech industry. As far as Oracle Corp. is concerned, this book reflects very much a business strategy still in the making. And my view of Larry Ellison continues to change.

For certain, I can say that he is not the "insubstantial" person that some members of the press have suggested he is. While I am uncertain whether I would like to work for this man, or for that matter spend more than an hour in his company, given the high energy he exudes, I can say that he has developed into a great manager and a great leader. Time and experience—good and bad—have erased managerial flaws, as happens with many of our best business leaders. Is Ellison an "oracle"? Yes, he has not only moments of "aha," creative ideas that he has successfully taken to the marketplace, but also the ability to recognize good ideas and ensure their successful commercialization. As someone who has long believed that an idea is of little value without successful implementation, it would be the latter talent I would extol.

But there is also another side to Larry Ellison, one that I hope this book demonstrates. There is a P. T. Barnum side to Larry Ellison. He took on the marketing role when Oracle was first launched. He took on the marketing role after its 1990 accounting crisis. And while he has assumed a more hands-on operating role within the company over the past few years, he continues to be the voice and face of Oracle, a spin doctor of Oracle's products and new services strategy. Which makes me wonder whether the well-publicized animosity between him and Microsoft Chairman Bill Gates was rooted more in a desire to gain the public's attention than any personal feelings about the man.

The Oracle of Oracle also carries a subtitle: "The Story of Volatile CEO Larry Ellison and the Strategies Behind His Company's Phenomenal Success." Yes, based on incidents in public and in private, Ellison is known for his volatility, both positive and negative. And ironically enough, he is taking his company into an area of business, the Internet, which is equally volatile, as the dot-com shakedown in the last two years has shown. Given our bumpy economy right now, the future of both Oracle and the Internet is uncertain and will likely continue to be reported by colleagues of mine in the press. This book, however, is designed to help the reader not only gain insights into Larry Ellison and Oracle, but also the software industry and management therein of fast-growth firms.

Florence Stone
September 2001

acknowledgments

I have done much writing in recent years about the high-tech industry, dot-coms, the impact of the Internet on legacy firms, and successful e-businesses. Throughout my research, the names Oracle Corp. or Larry Ellison seemed to arise frequently. After a brief period spent learning a little about this larger-than-life man and the company he launched, I couldn't resist the urge to pursue in-depth study of both for the purposes of a book.

So the idea for *The Oracle of Oracle* was born.

But this book could not have become a reality without the assistance of the many, many people in the software and investment communities who shared expertise about the software industry and observations about Larry Ellison and

Oracle. I am not the first person who has written about Larry Ellison, nor do I expect to be the last. I would be negligent if I failed to thank the following authors for the insights and information I gained from their books: Mike Wilson, author of *The Difference Between God and Larry Ellison: Inside Oracle Corporation;* Stuart Read, author of *The Oracle Edge;* David A. Kaplan, author of *The Silicon Boys and Their Valley of Dreams;* Mark Barrenechea, author of *E-Business or Out of Business: Oracle's Roadmap for Profiting in the New Economy;* Charles G. Sigismund, author of *Champions of Silicon Valley: Visionary Thinking from Today's Technology Pioneers;* and Detlev J. Hock, Cyriac R. Roeding, Gert Purkert, and Sandro K. Lindner, coauthors of *Secrets of Software Success.* Nor can I forget the numerous reporters, online and print, who have covered Larry Ellison and Oracle since its creation more than twenty-five years ago. Their tales, insights, and perspectives on these two Silicon Valley icons have made this book possible.

Finally, I would like to thank my wonderful editors at AMACOM: Christina McLaughlin, development editor, for her help in transforming a raw manuscript into the one I really meant to write; James Bessent, associate editor, for his remarkable attention to so many details that matter; and Adrienne Hickey, executive editor, for her patience during a very tough year as well as for her earlier support.

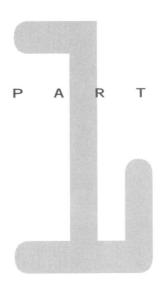

A MAN, A COMPANY,
A PLACE LIKE
NO OTHER

CHAPTER ONE

A BRIEF HISTORY

Larry Ellison and the company he made

Ruthless, volatile, arrogant, impatient, auto-cratic—all these adjectives have been used to describe Larry Ellison. I would agree, but I would add adjectives like insightful, customer-centric, and focused. In other words, Larry Ellison has all the traits and characteristics that make for an outstanding leader in the high-tech industry. He also has one characteristic that many lack—the ability to sell his ideas to others.

It is for this reason that I think of Ellison as the 21st Century's P. T. Barnum. Some reporters may have made the comparison because of his past history of unkept promises and half-truths. But to me he is like the P.T. Barnum in the play *Barnum*. If you saw that play, you will recall the song Barnum sings about two-thirds into the musical in which he describes himself as the "prince of humbug" and defines his "lies" as "rosy possibilities." Likewise, Ellison. But his rosy possibilities are cutting-edge technology to solve customers' problems.

Ellison's business persona has become so intertwined with his personal life that it is impossible to separate them, even in a business book whose purpose is to share the reasons behind Oracle's success. So as you read this, you will likely think about the many headlines that circle around this Technicolor executive. Who is the real Ellison?

Is Ellison a loser who was fortunate enough to be at the right place at the right time? Or is he someone who had a goal—to be president of his own company—and took advantage of an opportunity when it arose to make that dream happen?

Did Ellison grow that young business on the ideas of others? Or did he have the wisdom to recognize the commercial value of those ideas before the competition and made money from selling his vision?

Is Ellison a liar, full of empty promises and half-truths? Or is Ellison just overly optimistic, too often believing his own humbug?

Is he a ruthless competitor, known to cripple and maim other companies and even personally attack their leadership? Or is he just a savvy businessman who takes on his company's competitors to ensure his firm retains its position as second largest software firm in the world?

Did Ellison jeopardize his company because he liked the VP of sales more than the bean counter and consequently ignored warnings prior to the 1990 cash flow problem that almost destroyed Oracle? Or was he just too wrapped up in growing the business to notice what was occurring?

Is he a womanizer who deserved to be sued for sexual harassment? Or is he a CEO who made the mistake of having an affair with a secretary who worked for his firm and had nothing personally to do with her termination?

Is Ellison the kind of man who is so engrossed in himself that he wouldn't give a thought to other people's tragedies? Or is he the person who mobilized Oracle's top development, consulting, and support staff to help rescue agencies, law enforcement, military and other branches of the federal government to restore systems and relocate facilities and personnel affected by the September 11 terrorist attack on the United States?

As I write this, my opinions about "the real Ellison" shift almost daily. However, I can say three things:

1. I don't think I would want to work for Ellison.

2. I am not sure I would want to be his friend, although I think he could be a loyal one provided he felt your friendship wasn't prompted by his position or wealth.

3. I *would* invest in Oracle, because I think Ellison's one damn good businessman. You have only to stay abreast of the business press to know this.

Despite the ups and downs of the economy, Oracle Corp. seems to bump along, keeping its balance much better than many high-tech organizations, including its competitors. But, then, the organization thrives on change. So does its founder and CEO, Larry Ellison. Indeed, Oracle's success is attributed by many to Ellison's unique talent to predict market demands before his competitors, sometimes ahead of the market itself. Consequently, investment managers refer to him as "the oracle of Oracle."

The term *oracle* originated in ancient Greece. It refers to someone of great knowledge or wisdom, a person to whom all others come for answers. In Silicon Valley, there is only one Oracle with a capital *O*, the $10 billion software developer, and only one oracle with a lowercase *o*, the oracle or idea man, Ellison. Actually, Ellison is better known for his prognostications of business trends and corporate opportunities for the software company than he is as its top executive.

Many attribute the success of Oracle, the company, solely to the ability of its CEO to make effective strategic decisions. However, it is attributable as well to Oracle's structure and to those who work for Oracle and successfully execute those strategies. The organization's entrepreneurial structure, with one leader clearly at the helm, and the business values—from "crush the competition" to "think strategically" to "lock in customers, lock out competitors"—that employees learn to follow, all facilitate the management process. With Ellison setting future direction based on high-payoff opportunities, the employees have a clear sense of priorities and can work effectively and efficiently to make Ellison's goal of making Oracle the number one company a reality.

To understand the thinking behind Oracle's operational guidelines, not to mention the flamboyant style that is Ellison's, we have to understand Ellison.

The Modest Beginnings of a Silicon Valley Star

Larry Ellison has said that he had to create his own business because he knew he hadn't the patience to work for anyone else. He would have had to accept the opinions of those he didn't respect to move up the corporate ladder, and there was no way that Ellison could do that. It was this attitude, too, that caused him to drop out of college.

"I have always had difficulty with conventional wisdom," he once told *BusinessWeek Online*. "Teachers would say certain things—and I wouldn't necessarily believe what they had to say.

> **Larry Ellison had to create his own business because he knew he hadn't the patience to work for anyone else.**

Just because they said it, and they were experts, and they were in authority did not automatically mean they were right."[1]

Ellison dropped out of college twice: first, at the University of Illinois at Urbana-Champaign after two years, and then at the University of Chicago, after a semester. In between attending school, he traveled to Berkeley where he worked as a programmer. In 1966, after he left the University of Chicago, he returned to California because he had nowhere else to go.

His disdain of "conventional wisdom" didn't help his relationship with his parents. He didn't get along well with them at all. Writers who have psychoanalyzed Ellison in print have suggested that his obsession with success was motivated by a need to get approval from his parents and aunt and uncle. His mother, unwed, had left him as a baby with his aunt and uncle, who adopted and raised him. Ellison repeatedly was told that he would not amount to anything. Although he talked often about being his own boss even as a kid growing up in Chicago, he has said he had no great desire to conquer the software industry and only got serious about building a company when he realized he had to feed himself. "I can recall running out of money between paychecks, and living on macaroni and cheese and rice. But I didn't take money very seriously until my late twenties, and I wanted to buy a house. I thought: If only I had a house—I had never lived in a house before. I had to figure out some way to make enough money to get a house."[2]

California, the Early Years

In California, Ellison did computer-related work for many big companies. Known today for his $7,000 Armani suits, he had Camembert tastes even then, but his earnings were more suited to a Velveeta budget. Married, he overspent, leaving his wife to figure out how to pay the bills. Money problems soon affected the marriage. Adda Quinn, the first of his three wives, suggested he visit a marriage counselor, which he did. She told one reporter that although the advice he received did nothing to salvage the marriage, he returned determined to

> Feigin recalls someone who was always talking. "You didn't have to agree with him—he enjoyed a good argument."

be successful. That same desire for success drives him even now, as one of the richest men in the world and CEO of the second-largest software company. According to Quinn, during those early years, Ellison was very frustrated. He told Stuart Feigin, a coworker, that he wanted to be president of a company, but he didn't know how to go about it.

Feigin was working at Amdahl Corp., then a high-tech start-up in Sunnyvale, California, when he first met Ellison, a new hire, in 1973. Feigin later became one of the first full-time employees of Oracle. Now retired from Oracle, Feigin is often asked by reporters to describe the man with whom he worked at Amdahl. Feigin recalls someone who was always talking. The subjects ranged from presidential politics to real estate, to books, to the stock market. "You didn't have to agree with him—he enjoyed a good argument." It would seem that Ellison was developing the glib communication skills that an entrepreneur needs to get buy-in to his thinking. It's a talent Ellison applied during Oracle's start-up and the purchase of its first database products and has continued to use in pursuing subsequent additions to the company's product lines, including most recently the introduction of its E-Business Suite. The ego that manifests itself in meetings with staff, customers, and the press was also there in the early days.

According to Feigin, Ellison talked about himself and "how wonderful he was, how smart he was, and how rich he was going to be."[3]

That Amdahl laid him off when money got short probably seemed, to Ellison, the worst thing that could have happened. Yet for Ellison, it was probably the best thing that could have happened. From Amdahl, he went to work for Ampex Corp., an audio and studio equipment company, also in Sunnyvale. There he met the two men who would be his partners in the founding of Oracle Corp.

Oracle's Three Founders

Most businesspeople today, even Oracle customers, don't really know much about Edward Oates or Robert Miner, although their involvement was critical to the firm in its early years. Oates was a career programmer who operated IBM mainframes in the Army, then worked for several years at Singer Business Machines before moving on to Ampex. Miner was also a programmer. After graduating from the University of Illinois, he went to work for the Public Health Service to fulfill his draft requirements, moved on to IBM, and then went overseas to build operating systems for Computer Sciences

Corp.'s customers. He returned to the United States to work for Informatics, and while there, he was asked by the firm to be its representative at Ampex. Ampex then recruited him to become a manager of its programming department.

Both Oates and Ellison worked for Miner; Oates joined the programming department one day after Ellison, who had demanded to be transferred to Miner's department because his supervisor was technically incompetent. "I refused to work for him."[4] While at Ampex, the three men worked together to develop the software for a project sponsored by the CIA that would enable an organization to store and retrieve enormous amounts of digital information. The CIA's name for the project was Oracle.

Ellison was regarded as a "good programmer"—he told his biographer, Mike Wilson, that he was "a great one"—but a subsequent job he took at Ampex in sales and marketing would seem just as suited to him based on his subsequent career. Comparing Miner and Ellison as programmers, Miner enjoyed the details associated with completing a complex software or technology project. Ellison, by contrast, while capable of doing that part of the work, wasn't challenged by it. Rather, he wanted to understand the implications of the technology to the customer's problem.

Eventually Ellison and Miner would come to run things at Oracle; and though Oates stayed on board, he sold his share of the business to Ellison because of personal financial problems. Ellison biographer Wilson observes, "Larry was looking at the horizon. Bob [Miner] was steering the ship." In this respect, they were very much like another set of high-tech partners: Steve Jobs and Steve Wozniak of Apple Computer, Inc.

As it became evident that the CIA would drop further work on its Oracle project, Oates moved on. So did Ellison. Miner stayed on with Ampex. Ellison went to work for Precision Instrument Company, where he became vice president. Precision Instrument decided to outsource software development, which prompted Ellison to contact his former colleagues, Oates and Miner, to ask them if they would like to form a software development company with Precision Instrument as their first customer. Ellison put in $1,200, or two cents a share. Miner and Oates each invested $400 for their part of the business. They went along with Ellison's plan, believing they could find other work if the scheme failed.

Ellison was head of the business because, Oates remembered, "Larry was the prime mover behind this thing. He had more chutzpah than the two of us combined."[5] Under the firm's new name, Software Development Laboratories, the three men received an advance from Precision of $50,000. David A. Kaplan, author of *The Silicon Boys and Their Valley of Dreams*, suggests that the new company's management style reflected a time in Silicon Valley when hype was more important than technological expertise. "The marketing tail would wag the product dog."[6] Ellison was the salesman; Miner and Oates were the software programmers. Initially the company did contract work for other firms. In 1976 IBM published a

report describing a database system that would allow customers to store and find the correct data with a few simple
questions. The whole picture changed for Ellison and his
team. Ellison saw commercial value that IBM apparently
didn't and was able to capitalize on it. (For details on IBM's
negligence see Chapter 4.)

Oracle, the Early Years

Early on, Software Development Labs changed its name to
Relational Software Inc.; then in 1982 it adopted the name of
its relational software, Oracle, as the corporate name. It
wasn't just because they wanted a livelier name. The company
didn't want to be a software development laboratory anymore.
An early Oracle employee told Ellison's biographer, "They
wanted to do a software package and sell it like a doughnut—
you know, sell the same thing over and over." [7]

Even as Miner and Oates and a new employee, Bruce
Scott, worked to build a minicomputer version of relational
database software, Ellison was visiting potential customers
selling the product. The Oracle database management program was only a drawing on a piece of paper, yet Ellison
already had potential clients lined up. Once the product was
completed, it was called Oracle, after the CIA product that
originated back at Ampex. Author David Kaplan wrote, "The
name also fit the cocksure attitude of the company leader." [8]

All new software programs have bugs that only become
evident upon installation. So it was with Oracle. It was an

achievement, nonetheless; one that couldn't have happened without Ellison's persistence. Furthermore, it was Ellison, the "oracle of Oracle," who first thought that the software should be able to run on all computer systems so that it was not applicable solely for IBM Corp. or Digital Equipment Corp. systems. This portability feature is what really interested chief information officers. Among its first customers was the federal government, including the CIA.

The Oracle database software was the firm's core product, and it sold it through a sales force directly to information technology (IT) managers and their staffs. Oracle's marketing department generated the leads. The nature of the license—term or perpetual—and the anticipated number of users

> Ellison was the bad cop, Miner the good cop. People wanted to be hired by Ellison but wanted to work for Miner.

determined the price. Despite the company's tremendous growth in the marketplace, Ellison worried that somebody else could take away business. This prompted a tough competitive style—the "crush the competition" attitude—for which Oracle is known today. Because Ellison understood how important it was to lock up a large share of the market early, he pushed to build the company to a certain size to survive any potential shakeout in the industry. One of the early ads for the company had a fighter jet labeled Oracle "plowing the road," strafing buildings with the names of the competitive firms written on them.

In terms of management, former employees recall, Ellison played the role of bad cop, Miner played the role of good cop. "It was Larry who hired, but it was also Larry who fired. People wanted to be hired by Ellison but wanted to work for Miner," recalled one employee. "Ellison believed that Miner was 'loyal to the people before the company.'" [9] Miner didn't like the crushing demands he placed on the engineers, Ellison recalled.

On the other hand, in both his personal and professional lives, Ellison put the company first. It affected his relationship over the longer term with Miner and over the short term with his second wife, who divorced him a little over a year after the company's launch.

Ellison as Top Salesman: Half-Truths and Empty Promises

Ellison spent those early years marketing not only Oracle's product, but also the whole idea of relational database management. Much is made of Ellison's habit of hyperbole. Maybe it is still true, as an early Oracle employee once put it: "Average technology and great marketing beat good technology and good marketing every day."[10] Certainly it was the case in the early years of Oracle's history. Even when the product didn't live up to all the promises Ellison made, Ellison would crow endlessly about the technology. That early customers could speak to Ellison, Miner, or Oates when they encountered a problem helped quiet the complaints. Besides, those who made the dang thing work acknowledged the major impact it had on data management.

To this day, many people attribute Ellison's initial success to luck—after all, it was IBM that had developed the initial specifications for database management systems. Yes, Ellison

> **Ellison went further, using a single idea to build a major business with chutzpah, ceaseless work, unrelenting optimism, and ruthless determination.**

was at the right place at the right time, but likewise he was the first to see the commercial application of IBM's development. Moreover, Ellison went further, using that single idea to build a major business with chutzpah, ceaseless work, unrelenting optimism, and ruthless determination.

Ellison's Competitive Spirit

All the traits Ellison is known for today were evident even in Oracle's early history—and not only outside the company, either. He was also the corporate cheerleader, setting technical goals for the engineers that demanded stretch. Yet they were goals the engineers met because Ellison refused to believe they were unable to do otherwise.

We know about his behavior toward competitive companies, but Ellison showed that same competitiveness in his personal relationships, too. For instance, he repeatedly had chin-up contests with Bob Brandt, one of the firm's software developers. A superior athlete, Brandt always won, but that didn't stop Ellison from trying to beat him. Feigin recalled a weekend bike ride with Ellison and his second wife when Feigin beat Ellison up a steep incline. For a while, there were no more bike rides. Then one day Ellison asked Feigin to go for a ride. "He left me in the dust," Feigin said. "He had been practicing."[11]

Going Public

On March 15, 1986, Oracle went public, one day before Microsoft Corp.'s initial public offering (IPO). Ellison's private income ballooned to $90-plus million. Miner, who headed up development, didn't do too badly, either. Many Oracle employees became millionaires on that day. Feigin, who had been unable to get a loan to purchase a home, found he had no problem after the IPO. According to a story told by Ellison, after twenty years working with Miner, Miner had two chores to do at the bank that day. One was to cash a check for a few hundred dollars; the other was to deposit the check for $2 million-plus from his share of the IPO. When he told the teller his intent, she called a bank official, who said Miner didn't have to wait in line—Ellison had already made an appointment with the bank's president to pay off Miner's mortgages and invest the money.[12]

Success Distracts

The company did so well that Ellison drifted away from the day-to-day operation. Maybe it was because Ellison had kept his promise to make himself and Oracle's partners rich. Or perhaps the marketplace had settled down, and Oracle had such a sure position within it, that Ellison eased up. He became immersed in the life of the rich playboy.

In the growth of a new business, invariably there are hiccups and belches that can derail less skilled management. Amazon.com almost ran out of money after its successful launch and the press was extolling it as "the only Web site making money." Even today, Amazon is fighting off doubters because of its failure to deliver profits. Dell Computer Corp. for a time strayed from its initial business model of marketing computers via telephone and began selling computers through chain stores; after all, the other computer manufacturers were doing so. The decision raised operating costs so high that it made a major dent in the bottom line. Likewise, Oracle experienced its first business burp in 1990.

Busy pursuing business not associated with Oracle, including a Los Angles–based magazine called *Buzz*, Ellison wasn't aware that sales personnel, to meet their quotas, were making deals for which there were no products and never would be—consequently labeled "vaporware"—or logging sales for which contracts were never signed. Oracle's stock value collapsed as questions arose about the company's reported sales revenue. (This mess, and Ellison's strategies for dealing with it, is covered in Chapter 7.)

The New Oracle—And Oracle of Oracle

Within a year of the 1990 events, Oracle was on the mend. Ellison made full use of two newly hired executives with experience in dealing with the problems of big business: Jeff Henley, who had been executive vice president and chief financial officer at Pacific Holding Co., joined Oracle in 1991 to bring more discipline to the operations side, as well as to reassure Wall Street and the investment community. Henley is now Oracle's chief financial officer. Ray Lane was another seasoned professional who came from Booz-Allen & Hamilton to head up sales. He moved up to become Oracle's president, a position he held until 2000. But it was the product development area that truly saved Oracle.

Oracle7 database software, which hit the market in 1992, was miles ahead of products from competitors IBM Corp., Informix Corp. (whose products are now a part of IBM), and Sybase, Inc. Oracle7 introduced the ability to manage text, video, audio, and other data through a set of loosely connected servers.

The experience also changed Ellison's priorities. From an earlier mind-set that accepted mediocrity in product, Oracle's CEO announced, " . . . [Q]uality is absolutely the right strategy to kill our competition."[13] Ellison recognized that to succeed as a start-up, Oracle needed both an entrepreneurial

CEO and people who thought as he did; but the company had now grown beyond that stage and needed the management systems and processes of a mature company.

Although revenue began an upward trend that continued through 1998—$1 billion each year until in 1998 it was at $7 billion, with nearly a billion dollars of that as profits—all was not well. By 1992, Ellison had come to the conclusion

> **Ellison recognized that Oracle needed the management systems and processes of a mature company.**

that his old partner Bob Miner had nothing more to contribute as head of development. Miner himself was miserable in the position. According to Miner's daughter, her father felt that he had too much money, he had too many people working for him and didn't know their names, and he was tired of working to make Ellison's promises good. She recalled her father laughing bitterly as they rode in a car together, listening to Ellison on the radio promising technology by a certain date. There was no way that he could make the deadline, Miner told his daughter. Being told the story by his biographer, Ellison said, "I pissed a lot of people off that way. Still do."

Ellison and Miner agreed that Miner would continue to work for Oracle heading up a group of techies—"elitist weirdos," Miner called them—who would tinker along with him on new speculative technologies.[14] Within two years, however, Miner would be diagnosed with incurable cancer and die. When Ellison learned about Miner's physical condition, he discounted it. Ever optimistic, he responded that either the doctors were wrong in their diagnosis or Miner would beat it. When Miner asked for Ellison's help, he contacted specialists in the field to help his former partner. Miner refused the recommended treatment, preferring to stay in California with his family than go to Memorial Sloan-Kettering in New York. When Miner died, he was still on Oracle's payroll, by order of Ellison, who continued to hope for his friend's recovery. Ellison was among those who gave eulogies for the unassuming programmer who worried that he was making too much money. The oracle of Oracle acknowledged how his former partner had worked to make Ellison's visions a reality.

Business Problems, Too

Oracle wasn't immune to business difficulties, either. There were further hiccups. In December 1997, economic problems in Asia, where Oracle had major inroads, prompted a 29 percent drop in Oracle's stock. It was a big financial loss for Ellison—more than $2 billion—but he was still financially secure, with more than $5 billion in income. However, employees whose bonuses were based on stock options weren't so lucky. When they needed the CEO's presence to rally them, Ellison was on a Caribbean cruise. Even as the stock took another nosedive and Ellison's personal fortune dropped another billion-plus dollars, Ellison was away.

When he refocused on the business, however, it was with a new vigor, one he had seemed to lose in the mid-1990s. Prompted by the small growth in Oracle's traditional software market—10 percent or so—and Microsoft's release of its SQL Server, which sold at a lower price to rival Oracle's database, Ellison announced his decision to launch browser-based applications for the Internet-wired world. A few years before, in 1995, Ellison had sparred with Bill Gates over the future of the PC at the European Information Technology Forum in Paris (see Chapter 7). Gates argued that PCs would remain the means by which people hooked into a unified network. Ellison saw what he called "network appliances" replacing PCs.

Ellison halted production on all non-Internet-enabled software. He "placed all his bets on the Internet without a safety net," observed Jennifer Glass, vice president of public relations.[15] Gates, in the meantime, had recognized the implications of Ellison's words and rushed to offer an alternative to Ellison's vision—cheaper PCs.

The effort led ultimately to a management change at Oracle and an "aha moment" for Ellison a year later.

In 1997, Ellison realized that he could command the $20 billion application market using the Web-enabled software his firm had begun to build for its network appliances. In spring 2000, Oracle released the first fully integrated applications suite. Grumblings from customers prompted revisions.

With Oracle11i, Ellison has said he should be able to grow sales by as much as 70 percent with an upturn in the economy. But Oracle, like many high-tech firms, is hurting. Total revenue fell 3 percent from 2000. Net income is down 8 percent to $865 million, and sales of Oracle's trademark database

> **If Oracle is to be the largest software company Ellison wants it to be, it has to take over the applications software market. Which means taking on not only Microsoft, but IBM as well.**

product, that grew 12 percent just a year before, are expected to be flat in 2001. Most important, application software sales dropped 24 percent, while SAP and Siebel Systems, Inc., two of Oracle's biggest competitors, have had gains above that.

The database business, which makes up about one-third of Oracle's revenue, is anticipated to increase only 15 percent a year from 2001 until 2006. If Oracle is to be the largest software company in the world, as Ellison wants it to be, it has to take over the applications software market. Which means taking on not only Microsoft, but IBM, too.

*　*　*

In the following chapters, you will learn about the management in place at Oracle that has enabled it to grow from scratch to the powerhouse it is today. Descriptions of the management strategies that guide Oracle make up much of this book. These strategies are from the mind of Ellison, who once told a reporter: "When you find errors in conventional wisdom—when everyone says A and A is not true—that is when you gain competitive advantage. Only a few times do you have to find errors in conventional wisdom to make a living."[16]

As you study the value statements by which Oracle operates, you may find many with which you agree and would like to see practiced at your own firm. Simplistic at one level, complex on another, but based on Oracle's history, they would seem an effective way by which to manage.

CHAPTER TWO

SILICON VALLEY

the setting for two oracles

Larry Ellison was born in Chicago, but he has lived in Silicon Valley since his early twenties. They say we are a product of our environment. If you are to understand this larger-than-life billionaire CEO of Oracle Corp., let alone his company, you need to understand the lifestyle of those who have succeeded in the high-tech industry, the "town folk" with whom Ellison works and plays, as well as the town in which he lives.

Welcome to Silicon Valley

Silicon Valley is located in the heart of northern California. While most of us know the name, we probably don't know its exact location or the origin of the name. Today, Silicon Valley covers most of Santa Clara County, southern San Mateo

County, and southern Alameda County. Named for the principal material used in manufacturing semiconductors, the area gained renown in 1912 among scholars and scientists at Stanford University, whose work led to the development of integrated circuits, semiconductors, and computers. In the late 1960s and 1970s, the area saw dramatic growth, with electronics companies sprouting almost daily. In 1971, a local engineer who was also editor of *Microelectronics News* coined the term Silicon Valley. The name stuck.

Remember the geeks we teased while in junior high school? They wound up in Silicon Valley. Scientists and engineers, not to mention venture capitalists, entrepreneurs, and entrepreneur wannabes have all gone there, drawn in part by the presence of major companies such as Apple Computer, Inc. and Intel Corp. and Hewlett-Packard Co. that have been in Silicon Valley for several decades. It's one giant factory town where each and every organization's goal is to make a

> **Remember the geeks we teased while in junior high school? They wound up in Silicon Valley.**

major change technologically. I have a friend who once lived there. We chatted recently. A business book agent, she tells me that each professor she meets today has a manuscript ready to pull out when he knows who she is. In Silicon Valley, she recalled, everyone has *at least* one business plan, most of which pay more attention to exit strategy than the first three years of business growth. Just as she is chased after by professors of management, entrepreneurs seek out the venture capitalists in their midst.

Silicon Valley isn't small, but from a business perspective it behaves like it is—that is, everyone knows about the other person's business's achievements. Talk is more often about the successes than the flops—like John Doerr's financing of Amazon.com through his venture capital firm Kleiner Perkins Caulfield & Byers or the social life of the "name" residents like Steve Jobs, one of the founders of Apple.

The Lifestyle of the Rich and Richer

If there were a TV show about the lives of the successful entrepreneurs in Silicon Valley it would be titled "The Rich and the Filthy Rich." Woodside, considered the Beverly Hills of Silicon Valley, may be the only community in the United States in which junior high school students are required to take a course in "How to Be a Millionaire" that includes, as first math assignment, how to spend $1 million, with pictures of all purchases with prices and expenditures plotted on a Microsoft Excel spreadsheet. But, then, many of these young boys and girls are the sons and daughters of the country's leading entrepreneurs and venture capitalists. They live in Silicon Valley because their parents work there.

According to David A. Kaplan, author of *The Silicon Boys and Their Valley of Dreams*, about 250,000 millionaires live in the Valley. He projects that every day, the Valley produces sixty-four new millionaires depending on the state of the economy.

This is not to say that everyone who lives in Silicon Valley is a millionaire. There are manual and clerical workers who earn five-figure salaries and, given the high costs of housing,

> **Junior high school students are required to take a course in "How to Be a Millionaire" that includes, as first math assignment, how to spend $1 million.**

live in converted garages that were home to many Silicon Valley business startups. But they are the exception. Silicon Valley residents are among the most affluent in the United States, even with the dot-com downfall and the rocky road of tech stocks. Besides headquarters for Oracle, Silicon Valley is home for Hewlett-Packard, Apple Computer, Intel, Kaiser Permanente, Compaq Computer Corp., Raychem Corp., Adobe Systems, Inc., Sun Microsystems, Inc., and most recently Microsoft Corp.'s new Silicon Valley Technology Center. The market value of all companies there is more than $1 trillion. In all, there are a little more than 6,300 high-tech companies employing almost 300,000 employees, give or take a layoff.

Software engineers are drawn to Silicon Valley not only by the stock options and the promise of instant wealth, but by a culture that appeals to creative types. There are weeks, especially before major releases, when these talented people must work twenty-four hours a day for consecutive days, bringing along sleeping bags so they can stay in the office. There is no special incentive for that kind of commitment. These creative engineers and designers and other entrepreneurial wannabes do it because of the financial rewards *and* their commitment to the same desire to make an impact on the world that motivates the heads of their companies—the McNealys (Sun Microsystems), Jobses (Apple Computer and Pixar Animation Studios), and of course the Ellisons.

Cheerleaders like Ellison build a sense of excitement that keeps employees on the job until the product is completed. When they succeed, they are made to feel special, members of the in-group in their organizations, maybe a goal they never could achieve during their school days.

In return for the 24/7 work life, engineers have the opportunity to prove their ideas and themselves not only to those who called them geeks, but to former geeks who have already proved themselves and now have huge fortunes and the resources of large organizations as a consequence. Even in smaller companies this is true.

The Valley Economy, Post-Millennium

Silicon Valley is known less for the up-and-comers than for the current movers and shakers in the high-tech industry. Even the state of the economy after the dot-com debacle has not caused Silicon Valley to lose all its luster. Yes, the Valley has undergone other economic roller-coaster rides, and it is unclear just how rocky this one will be. Some long-term residents have sent e-mail to old friends about positions elsewhere, but there is always talk about new developments which lends an optimistic air.

Prior to September 11, 2001, research at most of the high-tech companies was on an increase, promising further developments in software, semiconductors, and networking equipment, and new developments in wireless communications and health-related products. The job market remained healthy. Unemployment was at 1.7 percent whereas new job development was growing at 4.4 percent—even with the economic slowdown, the demand for talented IT professionals continues to be high in Silicon Valley. Yet there is concern that the continuing flow of talent that Silicon Valley needs will choose to go elsewhere. Beyond that, the Valley's reputation as the birthplace of technological innovation is at stake. The area doesn't just draw entrepreneurs from the United States, either. Stephan Schambach founded Intershop Communications, a developer of graphic Web browsers, in eastern Germany, but following release of his company's first product, Schambach moved to Silicon Valley. He realized that he needed to be at the center of the world's rising electronic commerce marketplace. Within a few months, he had started a Silicon Valley subsidiary and made it Intershop's headquarters.

Among the products invented in Silicon Valley were the integrated circuit, the first commercial radio broadcast, video games, minicomputers, microcomputers, gene-splicing, 3-D computing, and Internet commerce. If further developments are to occur, the leaders in Silicon Valley want them to happen in their companies, so residents are working harder, giving greater attention to their company's strategic goals.

But playtime continues. And, interestingly enough, the same executives who spar in public are known to party at exclusive events, including on a few occasions Bill Gates and Larry Ellison. In the high-tech industry, companies behave like great pals and snarling enemies at the same time. A case in point: In 1996, as Oracle announced its Network Computer, Inc. subsidiary (now spun off as Liberate Technologies), it also announced that four major high-tech companies were joining it to develop open technological standards for network computers. The companies—IBM, Apple Computer, Sun Microsystems, and Netscape Communications—had all sent representatives to the event. In newspaper reports, the group was referred to as the anti-Microsoft coalition. At least for the day, these companies had united against a common enemy. On other occasions, they have been some of Oracle's bitterest rivals. IBM, for example, was a relational database rival. Ellison had little respect for Apple's then-CEO Gil Amelio, comparing him poorly to his personal friend Steve Jobs. And in the case of Netscape, Ellison had gone on record that it was overrated, both as a Web browser and as a stock.

Pickup Trucks and Mansions

In Silicon Valley, the economy hasn't influenced personal spending among the rich and famous. The residents of Silicon Valley seem out to prove that there is no such thing as too-conspicuous spending, but they don't seem to spend on transportation. Maybe to prove that they aren't completely materialistic, residents can be seen behind the wheel of pickup trucks. Ellison himself drives a Jeep (when he isn't driving his McLaren, Acura NSX, or Bentley turbo convertible, or flying his assortment of planes). Houses and entertainment are another matter. Residents of Silicon Valley seem to want the world to know just how rich they are. So there are the very elegant, very expensive parties for the in-crowd and local restaurants where you can purchase ostrich sausage for $15 a pound—and people do.

Perhaps most visible is the competition among Silicon Valley's successful entrepreneurs to own a bigger, better home than the next person. Fort Knox–type gates can be found to

> **Residents of Silicon Valley seem to want the world to know just how rich they are.**

keep out both the press and the curious, not to mention more nefarious visitors. The wife of an engineer from one of the Valley companies has a forty-eight-foot rack on which to hang her clothes. Then again, Mike Markkula, Jr., once one of Apple's senior executives, has enough room on his property to garage forty-two cars. Steve Jobs, Apple's cofounder, has two homes in the Valley—one for guests such as the president of the United States and the First Lady, and one for himself in Palo Alto. T. J. Rodgers, CEO of Cypress Semiconductor Corp., has his own winery on his property. In this competition, too, for who has the best home, it looks like the winner will be Ellison.

A $40 Million Conceit?

Despite the wobbliness of high-tech stocks, work is continuing on Ellison's twenty-three-acre, Japanese-style imperial villa. Since work first started in 1996, the earlier estimated cost of $40 million is no longer the case. It will cost closer to $80 or $100 million, which will make Ellison's Woodside, California mansion the priciest, if not most exclusive, in the area. "It's unique in magnitude, materials, and architectural design," the town's planning director, David Rizk, has said.[1]

Builders relocated enough earth to build an entire football field in order to create the estate's ponds, hills, and islands. A 2.7-acre main pond with a 3,200-foot-long shoreline will be fed by two waterfalls cascading from another pond, about a half acre in size. More than 500 trees—cherry and maple—have been planted to supplement about 700 existing redwoods, pines, oaks, and other species. And to re-create Japanese-style gardens, thousands of shrubs and several tons of boulders have been hauled in. In all, there will be ten buildings, including a main residence with three wings connected by walkways and an underground parking garage; a teahouse; moon pavilion; guest house; bridge house; boathouse; barn; and "Katsura house," which is a made-in-Japan replica of a teahouse built as part of a royal compound of the same name in Kyoto, Japan, in the 1600s.

When construction first began, one reporter dubbed it a "$40 million conceit." Even while it may be the biggest home in Silicon Valley, it isn't the largest home in high-techdom. That's owned by Bill Gates, Microsoft's CEO, whose Medina, Washington home is 48,160 square feet and is being expanded. If he could have done so, Ellison likely would have built his mansion at least to that size, but there is a firm 8,000-square-foot limit on a main residence in Silicon Valley.

In the high-tech world, size is important—particularly between these two men.

In the late 1980s, Ellison had just completed work on his huge home in Atherton. It had cost him a few million dollars. He had bought and remodeled a mansion after the Katsura Villa in Kyoto. The house had white oak floors, shoji screens on the windows, a gallery where Ellison could display his collection of antique Kabuto helmets, and a Japanese tea ceremony room. One day, he had a call from Bill Gates. He wanted to stop by and "talk about stuff," Ellison recalled.[2]

There was no competition between the two businesses back then; one company built database software, the other wrote operating systems and applications for PCs. Nor was there any competition or animosity between the two men, although some people have suggested that Ellison resented the fact that Oracle's IPO success had been outshone by Microsoft's IPO the next day. Ellison sent Ed Oates, one of Oracle's cofounders, to meet Gates's plane at the San Francisco airport. Oates led him to a Porsche 911 Turbo Cabriolet, a small but very expensive convertible; Oates thought Gates would appreciate the drive since he was awaiting his own Porsche, a 959—that's right, a more expensive model. When they got to Ellison's home, Oates left Gates with Ellison.

As Ellison took Gates on a tour of his home, he found he liked him, he later told his colleagues. He also admitted that he had talked on and on while Gates just listened. Ellison is known for his stream of consciousness communication even

> **Gates told Ellison that he thought Ellison's house "was cool." Then he added, "I'm building a bigger one."**

today. At the time, he tried to tell himself to shut up—this wasn't like talking to a customer or a senior member of his own management team. After the fact, Ellison realized that Gates had been on an intelligence-gathering mission, curious to see if Ellison and Oracle might have plans that would put them on the same course as Gates and Microsoft.

The punch line that also tells you something about the highly competitive players in the high-tech industry is this: Just before his departure Gates told Ellison that he thought Ellison's house "was cool." Then he added, "I'm building a bigger one."[3]

Ellison couldn't ignore the challenge: He drove Gates back in his Ferrari Testarossa.

Why am I telling this story? It isn't to prove that Bill Gates started this rivalry. It is to give you insight into the competitive personalities of those who head up our high-tech companies. Just as competitiveness is very much a characteristic of the companies in the industry, it is a trait of those who are leaders in the industry. Otherwise, they would not have reached those positions.

The New Economy's Leaders

Interestingly, both Ellison and Gates are very much alike, and also very different from earlier leaders in the high-tech industry—and earlier residents of Silicon Valley. Hewlett-Packard founders Bill Hewlett and David Packard had goals beyond making bundles of money and controlling the marketplace— they were as motivated to provide job security, build world-class products, and satisfy customers. They were the kind of men who flipped a coin to decide whose name would come first in the corporate name. Gates possesses a desire to rule the market and tangential markets the way Ford, Rockefeller, and Carnegie did more than a century ago. Ellison seems simply motivated by a desire to win, with money as a yardstick for success, which consequently should be flaunted.

Besides, these days it is very much a part of the role of CEO of a high-tech firm to be a high-profile, high-adrenaline personality.

The CEOs of leading high-tech companies are well-known personalities. After all, there are many companies demanding the attention of the marketplace, and a high-profile CEO can help separate his or her company from the herd—whether it is Bill Gates, Hasso Plattner of SAP, or Larry Ellison. Public relations is necessary because attackers are always on the sidelines waiting to break into the market and take over the alpha's position in the pack. Because of Microsoft's PR, no one would have used the term "ruthless" to describe Bill Gates—at least until Microsoft was brought to court and accused of monopolizing the high-tech industry. Rather, he was perceived as leader of the nerds but a guru, an executive who took time in 1997 to sit down with a class of twenty junior high school students in California to talk about the "future of technology." He not only chatted with them, but also surfed the Web as cameras captured the moment. SAP's Plattner has written a book, which isn't bad PR for his firm, but he has been good at PR for years. Who in the software industry could forget Plattner's guitar playing on stage at the 1995 SAP Sapphire user conference with more than 4,000 IT experts from thirty-one countries in the audience? The media loved it, and Plattner—and his firm—consequently got lots of trade publicity.

Ellison also has become a recognized brand as a manager, leader, and visionary as I discuss in detail in Chapters 9 and 10.

Take his win at the helm of his yacht *Sayonara* in the Sydney Big Boat Challenge, or his near-death experience on the same boat. His boating successes have struck gold for Oracle—even the story that followed his win in the 1996 Miami to Montego Bay sailboat race. The story goes that Roy Disney, nephew of Walt, made fun of Ellison's boat, even suggesting he not bother to set sail. Ellison not only sailed, he won by several hours. And thereafter—he says many, many hours later—he boarded one of his planes and flew it down to about fifty feet over the water, throttled up to 250 knots, and went right between Disney's boat and another boat. He then pulled up as hard as he could and turned right in front of both boats. He told the press that it was perfectly legal—he was in international waters. "It was one of those wonderful immature acts for which you can't pass up the opportunity," he said to the press, grinning.[4]

All right, you say. It's a lot of publicity for Oracle. But what about the other situations that Ellison has been associated with—such as landing his plane at the San Jose airport without approval from the tower, or taking late-night flights over Gates's home to buzz the Microsoft CEO? How about his placing an ad for a wife (it was a joke for the three-time married executive)? And how about that MiG the press says he bought to strafe Gates's home? First and foremost, the Valley brings together strong-willed personalities in social and business situations. Their success gives them a sense of freedom that most of us lack—but would wish for. Second, like the Old

West of an earlier generation, Silicon Valley is a bigger-than-life mindset that contains some admirable moments, some hyperbole or downright lies, and lots of fun for lots of big kids. Indeed, Ellison would seem like a character from one of those 1940s or 1950s Western movies, but rather than wear a white hat throughout the movie he periodically changes to a darker version of the same hat (not black) to win in the final gunfight.

> **Silicon Valley is a bigger-than-life mindset that contains some admirable moments, some hyperbole or downright lies, and lots of fun for lots of big kids.**

Tom Peters said, "We have a ludicrously unfair share of the world's demented dreamers, all gathered in Santa Clara County." Peters continued, "The most demented of these is Larry Ellison. I think he's just fabulous. He doesn't have a single screw in place, and that puts him in damn good company."[5]

Management Analysis

The story of Larry Ellison isn't one of rags to riches. He came from a middle class environment, after all. But the distance in lifestyle from Chicago to Silicon Valley is substantial—and not solely based on the dollars in his bank account. In building a successful business, he has proven himself to fit within the ranks of the Hewletts and Packards, the Gateses and the Jobses.

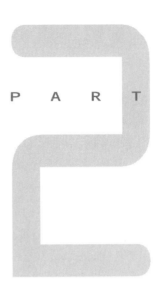

ORACLE'S VALUE SYSTEMS AND STRATEGIES

CHAPTER THREE

THE SPIRIT
BEHIND
ORACLE

would you want to
work for this man?

Over the years, I've studied numerous companies. In almost each occasion, I have found the culture and business philosophy to be a reflection of the founder and chief executive officer. Oracle is no exception. The idea to market database software as a product that would run on multiple computer platforms came from its visionary CEO, Larry Ellison, and subsequent product lines have stemmed very much from his understanding of the business marketplace and customer needs. Likewise, Oracle's corporate culture and approach to recruitment and performance management are reflections of elements in Ellison's personality. Aspects of his drive, ambition, and style have created the image that is Oracle.

When you study a company as I have Oracle, you find yourself unsure whom to believe. Ellison's flamboyant personality and history as a ruthless competitor makes it difficult to figure out just what working for this man is like. Ellison is infamous for cavalier firings and for burning top lieutenants. Thomas Siebel, a former Oracle executive and founder and

> People who are control oriented are perfectionists, driven by a vision that they expect you to accept if you work for them. Ellison is so driven.

CEO of Siebel Systems, Inc., an Oracle competitor, once said: "Larry doesn't foster a lot of loyalty. People stay at Oracle because they are well paid and fear recrimination. But Larry is a control freak. He has a knack for taking the best and the brightest—and then he tries to destroy them." David Rouz, an Ellison friend and former Oracle disciple, dismisses the complaint, pointing to the fact that many of Oracle's defectors end up competing against Ellison. Says Rouz: "Larry Ellison is a silver-backed gorilla alpha male. He will respond to a direct challenge, but only to a direct challenge."[1]

Control freaks are control-oriented alpha personalities in their demeanor. They are perfectionists, driven by a vision that they expect you to accept if you work for them. Ellison is so driven. The Ellison personality—private as well as professional—is very much part of the organization's value system. His strong will has enabled Oracle to adapt quickly to shifting market demands and sudden competitive threats—quicker even than more structured organizations. A highly visible, committed leader also ensures speedier alignment with a new approach (think "e-business software"). In short, where Larry leads, all others are expected to follow. Those who don't follow tend to move on, to found their own businesses (e.g., Siebel), become heads of major tech firms (e.g., Gary Bloom, CEO of Veritas), or be scooped up by a venture capitalist (e.g., Ray Lane).

Ellison's dream is built on a need to prove to the world that he is successful, and proof of that need is evident from the first time you enter corporate headquarters.

The Look of Success

There is no better way to understand the company's character—indeed, to understand its founder, Larry—than to visit 500 Oracle Parkway in Redwood City, California. When Oracle bought land in Redwood Shores in the late 1980s to build a new headquarters for the fast-growing software company (it had outgrown its earlier location), Ellison contracted with an architect for "a gleaming monolith in a Japanese garden." The look he wanted would not only reflect his interest in Japanese culture and samurai lifestyle he so admired, but it also would be representative of a successful company with its pulse on the future. Made mostly of green glass, the buildings were designed to stand as a monument to Oracle's past successes and future accomplishments. In the beginning, there were two large structures. As Oracle has prospered, the complex has grown. Four towers have been added, along with the complex's own utility station, surrounding a manmade lake.

The story goes that as additional towers were built, Ellison chose to relocate himself at the top floor of the tallest structure in the campus, in the swankiest office there. Ellison is a living icon for the company. The elegant structure at 500 Oracle Parkway, with its manicured grounds changed to reflect the seasons, is an icon too, one designed to impress potential customers and partners as well as make prospective employees feel good about working for this company. This purpose may explain the major investment in maintaining the headquarters.

Image is important to Ellison personally, but he also sees it as critical to doing savvy business. So the offices of Oracle themselves are also very different from the utilitarian, egalitarian appearance of the suites of most high-tech firms. Yes, there are posters of Oracle ads that show its products' performance against those of chief competitors, but there is also original art, Japanese and other, that is shuffled about regularly to keep employees from becoming bored by the same view day after day. The furniture isn't the kind one would find in a Steelcase catalog; the inner offices are yuppified with expensive furniture and designer offices for favored employees. There is a football field–size gymnasium to help employees stay fit; dining facilities of expensive hardwood and stylized stainless steel that offer a variety of ethnic food and even provide take-home dinners for employees pulling a late-nighter; and Ellison's own regal suite. All have been assembled to suggest affluence—and attract major corporations as clients.

Dress to Impress

That same look of affluence is expected of those within the company. For Ellison, who always appears trim and dashing in Italian suits and ties, both of which he wears in a style that belies his fifty-seven years, appearance is critical—and that philosophy extends to his workforce. If you work for Oracle, you may not wear an Armani suit like Larry, but you wouldn't come into the office in business casual, either. Oracle wants

> **By the look of your clothing, by the condition of your briefcase, by the state of your office, by the year and model of car you drive, you communicate your position—so Oracle employees learn.**

its employees to look and dress well—not only must they be in good physical shape, but they should dress to make a good impression on those with whom they come into contact. By the look of your clothing, by the condition of your briefcase, by the state of your office, by the year and model of car you drive, you communicate your position—so Oracle employees learn. Remember how your mom told you always to wear clean underwear because you never know. . . At Oracle, the message is somewhat the same: Dress to impress, since you never know when someone from outside may visit. Always look your best. At Oracle headquarters you will find tailored salespeople and, yes, even programmers. Even those who communicate with customers solely via telephone are "dressed for success."

Long Hours

This concern about image extends beyond the superficials of office furnishings, décor, and staff wardrobes. When it comes to job performance, Ellison and his management team will not tolerate mediocrity—they realize the cost for not getting it right the first time in the highly competitive database software market, whether it is in a product or in promotional literature about that product. On one occasion, Ellison paid $50,000 to redo an annual report because he didn't like his quote on the front page. This story is among the many Ellison stories told to new recruits to send the message to each generation of hires how perfection is the standard that is expected of them.

The company knows there is a cost—hard work and long hours. At a time in business history when companies are concerned about the balance between work and family, Oracle bucks the work/life trend. It believes in its employees putting in long hours if a project demands it. It is a measure of employees' dedication, a factor that can make a difference in whether Oracle has the better product available first. Stuart Read recalls a conversation with a department head while he was at Oracle. The manager told Read, "The schedule here is flexible. You can work any hours you want—but don't kid yourself—it's sixty hours a week."[2]

If you measure Oracle employees' work ethic by "the parking lot test," says Read, they would clearly pass.[3] What is the parking lot test? Read learned about it from a venture

> At a time in business history when companies are concerned about the balance between work and family, Oracle bucks the work/life trend.

capitalist who used it to evaluate start-up companies. After looking through a business plan for a new business, the venture capitalist said that he would make an effort to drive by the company's offices and check out the parking lot. The more employee cars in the corporate parking lot late at night and on the weekend, the more likely the employees were committed to the corporate vision and not consumed solely by the matter of pay. There are plenty of cars in Oracle's lot after 8 P.M. on weeknights, according to Read.

This matter of putting in long hours is even a part of the Oracle success story. The company had not yet gone public, and Ellison and his partners and their small staff were working out of an incubator on Sand Hill Road, staying late night after night "desperate to make good on the product promises that Larry had made," according to Read.[4] Nearby were the offices of a prominent venture capitalist who also was working late those nights. As the VC left one night, he noticed the lights on in the office and cars in the parking lot. On subsequent evenings, he looked to see if the lights were on. And night after night, they were. He assumed that such hard work meant Ellison and his team had to be working on something important. When Oracle needed external funding, this venture capitalist was one of the few who made himself accessible to Ellison and his partners.

Performance Management

This dedication is well rewarded. Ellison isn't the only person who has become rich from the company, although it is hard to ignore all it has given him: three Bay Area homes, a giant $50,000 plasma-screen TV, a koi pond full of personally named specimens, a brown Bentley convertible, a Porsche Boxster, two customized Mercedes, a Jeep, an $875,000 McLaren Roadster, a Gulfstream 5 fighter from Italy, a Cessna Citation jet, a bunch of acrobatic planes, a hanger for staff with lounge, and most noteworthy a lavish mansion under construction. Until 2000, Oracle had made Ellison the second-richest man in the world. Even with the topsy-turvy high-tech industry, he is still one of the richest men in the world—number five by the last *Forbes'* report.

Those who can tolerate the long hours and a work culture that won't settle for anything short of great can become millionaires themselves. Stuart Feigin, who was one of the first programmers at Oracle, was able to retire a multimillionaire before he was fifty.

Raises and bonuses are based on annual assessments, but these assessments aren't typical of those done in most companies in which employees get rated and are accordingly rewarded. At Oracle, the review process is designed to identify those with the ability and talent to move up, those who can remain where they are, and those who should be reassigned or encouraged to leave. Managers have a pool of money, according to Read, and at least 10 percent of any group received no raise or bonus during the early 1990s when he was at Oracle. The majority of those within a group got

> **Those who can tolerate the long hours and a work culture that won't settle for anything short of great can become millionaires themselves.**

raises and bonuses below average. Star employees received raises, bonuses, and stock packages that exceeded annual compensation. In Read's viewpoint, "When it comes to employees with good ideas, Oracle definitely plays favorites. These employees are richly rewarded while others are overlooked or terminated."[5] The goal is to encourage those who are judged above-average to set the standard, to encourage those judged average to work harder to equal that standard, and to help those who received nothing to recognize that Oracle isn't for everybody.

Based on their manager's evaluation, junior staff members may find themselves not only with bigger bank accounts but also greater corporate stature and new responsibilities. Along with performance evaluations, Oracle annually undergoes a reorganization process in which staff members are moved up or over to another position or judged dispensable. During Read's seven years with Oracle, he recalls that he had seven positions and twenty-two managers.

About 25 percent of employees get a different position or a new manager as a consequence of reorganization. Admittedly, this Oracle tradition has its shortcomings as well as benefits. On the plus side, it offers new recruits the opportunity to advance quickly and be compensated accordingly if they

> Oracle undergoes an annual reorganization process in which staff members are moved up or over to another position or judged dispensable.

demonstrate the talent the company needs. Consequently, it helps to attract and retain the very best. This organizational shakeup can change circumstances even for average workers who may not do well under one manager yet may excel under another. On the other hand, with each job there would seem to be a learning curve. And knowledge is lost as a developer moves on to another project, without the information that the previous job holder had. Intellectual capital has to be re-created year after year as developers move up or across to other projects. For the most part Oracle operates through and by teams, but often the teams are shattered during reorganization. Those who come to Oracle discover that the secret of succeeding within or outside the team environment is to learn how to operate successfully in a workplace without a structure of its own. It is up to the person to create that structure. These circumstances add pressure as one takes on new assignments, pressure that can distract an employee from the job itself.

There would seem also to be a tendency for the staff to be very competitive to ensure that they get labeled "star" material. Staff members want to be assigned to high-visibility projects where they have the opportunity to shine. That may explain why WebFeet's *Insider's Guide* on Oracle mentions a competitive spirit among staff that sometimes interferes with work getting done.

There is another problem with reorganization: Since it can occur before completion of a project, it also would seem to let an employee with a good idea be well rewarded, then move on, before that idea is tested. The individual who tests the idea may be labeled "average" if the idea fails to achieve the results promised, but the person with the initial idea may be long gone, depending on the length of time it takes to complete the project.

What if you aren't deemed able to move up or over to another challenging project but are found not to be suitable for your current position? If the manager believes that you would still fit well within Oracle, you might be sent home while the manager looks for a position for you. That the employee is asked to leave during this period is designed to reduce the effect of emotional turmoil on the work.[6] This period can last as long as thirty days. If no opening is found, the employee is notified immediately and terminated with two weeks' notice.

Oracle is obviously a tough place to work—despite the fine layout and furnishings. Given this work environment, where does it find prospective hires?

Recruitment

Clearly, Oracle wants to hire the very best. Keep in mind that Ellison's company's success is very much a reflection of his drive to succeed. And he wants to surround himself with those who possess similar drive. Mark Jarvis, senior vice president of marketing, speaks about both the company's culture and character with pride. He isn't the only Oracle employee who has told me how the company, launched a little more than twenty-five years ago, still offers the energy and excitement of a start-up yet provides the opportunities of a Fortune 500 corporation. The culture of the business is competitive and aggressive, so job hunters in need of a nurturing, supportive work environment should look elsewhere.

Techies aren't the only kind of employee that Oracle wants.

While it has a continuous need for talented technical personnel, there is also room for nontechnicians. Indeed, unlike many high-tech firms, Oracle considers nontechies equally as important to the company's future. First and foremost, the company wants people with intelligence and ambition.

If you have the first quality, intelligence, you know when to question an idea or move forward with one. If you have the second quality, ambition, you will be willing to put in the long

> **First and foremost, the company wants people with intelligence and ambition.**

hours that Oracle demands of its people. Because you will have lots of tasks, Oracle employees tell me, you will need to know how to prioritize. And to move from an idea to results, you will need strong networking skills. Networking skills are critical because Oracle is primarily divided along functional, not product, lines, so employees must have solid relationships with people in the other divisions to stay on top of things.

Oracle doesn't have any preset career paths, so employees are expected to chart their own path. That path can be vertical or, depending on how you measure up, it can be horizontal. Talented employees have been known to start in one division, declare their dislike (or unsuitability) for a work area where they find themselves, and be able to move over to a different job where they excel.

In the final assessment, talent is valued at Oracle.

ONLY THE VERY BEST

According to Roger Bamford, one of the organization's early top programmers, "When the company was launched, the favorite interview question on university campuses was, 'Are you the smartest person here?' A negative answer prompted a follow-up question: 'Well, who is?' That, then, was the individual the recruiter went after."[7] In other words, as in most things that have to do with Ellison or Oracle, neither will settle for second best. Both are on the look out for number one. In this instance, it is the job candidate with the most poten-

> **Neither Ellison nor Oracle will settle for second best.**

tial. This is why entry-level recruitment is still from the very best of schools, such as Brown, CalTech, Harvard, MIT, and the University of California at Berkeley.

On the other hand, Oracle does not limit itself to college graduates. How could it? After all, its own CEO was a dropout. In fact, some of the top executives in the high-tech field were dropouts, including Bill Gates and Michael Dell.

Oracle's indifference to a sheepskin may separate the company from many high-tech firms today. There is a story that would seem to prove this. In summer 2000, the staff of an online recruiter decided to test the capability of human resources managers to separate the wheat from the chaff among job applicants. They placed job ads for two executives using backgrounds very similar to those of Microsoft's Bill Gates and Oracle's Larry Ellison. Although neither ad received a response, the story got much press, and it may have prompted either a fabricated story about Ellison or a real-life incident involving Ellison during a commencement address at Yale.

Dressed in cap and gown, so the story went, Ellison told Yale's year 2000 graduates that they were "losers" whose hard-won diplomas would never make them rich. All their diplomas could give them were "pathetic $200,000-a-year jobs where your checks will be signed by former classmates who dropped out two years ago."[8] News stories suggest that Ellison was unceremoniously escorted off the stage.

What happened? Either it was a joke by Ellison or a joke on him. A company spokesperson told me it was a lark by Ellison.[9] Whatever, many members of the press reported it as "news," thereby pointing to the danger of a high-profile personality who gets his kicks by periodically playing up his "bad boy" image.

WINNING CHARACTERISTICS

A college diploma isn't essential, but it doesn't disqualify you to work for Oracle, either. Whichever your background, however, there are specific traits and characteristics that Oracle looks for. Over the years, recruitment at Oracle has evolved into a science of sorts. First, the company wants those with the ability to communicate effectively. In particular, Oracle wants individuals who are able to articulate their ideas to others and can consequently build a collegial team to attack problems. Intelligence is a given. So is a sense of humor. Finally, the company wants those with the same compulsiveness about reaching set goals that their own CEO has. That may explain the need for humor—to temper all those egos.

Once hired, employees undergo an orientation that extends beyond the usual hour at most companies and full day at more progressive companies. The orientation training at Oracle can last from three to six weeks for some new hires. During this time, candidates learn about and practice the values important to Oracle. Take competitiveness. From day one, employees compete in teams to create a product using Oracle technology.

> **Job candidates need communication skills, a sense of humor, and a compulsive need to reach set goals.**

It is also a time for recruits to build their first people networks to help them in the future. One Oracle employee told me that the early ties can be so strong that teams come back for reunions for many years thereafter. The sessions are Oracle's form of "boot camp," and those who have experienced it point to how it cuts as much as six months from the learning curve about Oracle products and enables new recruits to take the first steps in creating an internal network of contacts that is critical to getting things done in Oracle. It also ensures that everyone within the organization is familiar with the organization's value system (see Chapter 1) as well as its structure.

Oracle's Organization

Organizationally, there are five divisions: sales, product development, education, consulting, and finance and administration. Decentralized, the divisions handle their own functional responsibilities. So, for instance, those in charge of software development have their own marketing and sales and administrative resources. Development is divided into server technologies, tools, and business applications. Ellison spends much of his time in development, although he continues to spearhead much of the firm's marketing/promotion campaigns as well. Contrary to the impression given by the press, Ellison is very much a hands-on executive, known as much in the company for working hard as for playing hard.

Consulting, education, and support services fill out the organization picture, added to the enterprise to ensure Oracle customers use its products to improve their businesses. In all, the company has more than 10,000 consultants around the world to share the company's story about products and services. (Chapter 5 on customer relationships explains more about this operation.)

SUCCESSION PLANNING

At present, there is no first mate, to use a nautical analogy, to Ellison's role as captain as he steers Oracle to the lead in the applications business. Once again, he is on his own. Two likely heirs resigned within months of each other in the year 2000, leaving him with only Executive Vice President Safra Catz to back him up. Ray Lane, hired from Booz-Allen & Hamilton to become chief operating officer and president in 1996, is now general partner with Silicon Valley venture capitalist Kleiner Perkins Caufield & Byers. Gary Bloom, formerly an executive vice president, became president and chief executive of VERITAS Software Corp. Bloom was once considered a likely heir to Ellison, and his departure raised serious concerns about succession planning. To Mark Jarvis and the other members of Oracle's senior management team, this isn't a management concern, despite the fact that the press has falsely reported that Ellison is considering retirement and even, like Paul McCartney of the Beatles, that he was dead. Oracle operates around a team of senior vice presidents, each responsible for a functional area, as Jarvis is responsible for marketing. Indeed, the organization as a whole is organized around the team concept, although individualism is appreciated and rewarded.

As far as Ellison is concerned right now, naming a successor "is a dumb idea."[10] Bloom's appointment to head VERITAS, already an Oracle partner, should bring the two organizations closer. Lane's move was another story, one that the business press milked, particularly when the former president and COO at Oracle announced he had joined the board of Asera, Inc., a private business with plans to make software packages work together more efficiency. In other words, he's working for a future competitor of Oracle. Lane felt that companies didn't want to wait for an Oracle package of applications.

Before his departure, Lane was instrumental in hiring seasoned professionals and growing both product and brand. He worked closely with Ellison to create a complete product line; to make Oracle, if not a household name, a name known in corporate corridors worldwide; and to assemble, train, and retain a strong sales force and managerial staff.

What really happened with Lane? Ellison committed his company to creation of an integrated "suite" of applications that would require no customization or costly installation since the software could be delivered over the Web and sub-

> **As far as Ellison is concerned, naming a successor "is a dumb idea."**

sequently managed by Oracle via the Internet. The applications would include human resources management, sales, and supply chain management. It was 1997 and Ellison told the press he would have the product available by the start of the new millennium (2000). As the date came closer and closer, Ellison began to take back control he had given Lane, beginning with control of the marketing group, likely on the assumption that his involvement would spur those working on the project to meet the deadline.

In her article in *Forbes*, Carleen Hawn suggests that Ellison's near-death experience aboard his yacht *Sayonara* in 1998, during which the rough seas forced him to turn over the boat to a professional, may have triggered his need for control and subsequent desire to call all the shots.[11] Besides the applications business, he was in control of development, marketing, and services, all of which reported either directly to him or through Catz. Ellison even insisted on involving himself in approval of licensing contracts.

Oracle made its deadline, releasing its first fully integrated applications suite (E-Business Suite) in the spring of 2000, but customers weren't happy with the product. It had too many bugs. Did Ellison attribute the problems to Lane's more mild-mannered style of management, or did he feel that Oracle's new direction required a single navigator? Ellison probably sees a major challenge before him, and while the task could benefit from a strong "number one," Ellison has chosen to steer this ship without the aid of a "professional," moved both by his vision and unwillingness to share the glory.

Management Analysis

Is naming a successor a dumb idea? At present, Ellison's selection of an heir would only complicate his stewardship of the organization. Transforming an organization into an e-business is a difficult effort at any time but more so given our economy. Rumor has it that Lane distracted from Ellison's leadership, so his departure has actually made the management of Oracle simpler given the smooth flow of communication between Ellison and his senior management team.

On the other hand, while Oracle may talk about a "team culture," and indeed teams are part of the structure of Oracle, rewards go to the brightest and most talented. This would seem to be behind the competitiveness among employees, a competitiveness that may even be promoted to get the most creative ideas from the engineers.

I can't help but think that Ellison sees his people as widgets, to be used then discarded as they burn out. Which isn't necessarily any different from lots of CEOs' view of their workforce.

CHAPTER FOUR

CRUSH THE COMPETITION

more than a marketing slogan

When people criticize Oracle's tough attitude toward its competitors, they seem to be suggesting that Oracle is the exception—that other companies like to have competitors out there taking away clients or cutting into their market share. Truth is, while today it may make business sense to "go to bed" with a competitor if it satisfies both firms' long-term objectives, business still is a matter of dog eat dog, and in high-tech companies perhaps even more so.

In his book *The Silicon Boys and Their Valley of Dreams*, Kaplan writes, "Silicon Valley is the geeks' El Dorado," and the billions of dollars that can be made there triggers greed, and that "greed fosters intense competition."[1] The competitive fighting at which Ellison is considered an expert would seem only natural.

It may also be required of Ellison to be a ruthless competitor in his position as Oracle's chief executive given the company's business. The software industry itself is viciously competitive.

Ellison even found himself being compared in the press to the villainous software company CEO Roger Corwin, played by Tim Curry, in the movie remake of the 1970s television series *Charlie's Angels*. Sony Pictures Entertainment, the film's distributor, denied the resemblance. Ellison laughed it off. No question, there were commonalities—from appearance to residence to mode of transport. Consider Corwin's "business mantra." In one scene, when someone refuses a business deal on the phone, Corwin replies, "Over your dead body? I can live with that." Ellison and Oracle haven't gone that far, but they are known to hammer at a firm until it closes its doors. Their assaults on the competition may be critical to survival in the hypercompetitive marketplace.

Press reports suggest that Oracle doesn't just want to beat competitors; they want to destroy them. Even when a competitor is on the ground, they don't stop until the organization has died—and therefore is no longer a threat.

Ellison once quoted Genghis Khan while speaking with a reporter: "It is not enough that I succeed; all others must fail."[2] Stuart Read, in his book *The Oracle Edge*, writes, "For Ellison, any business tolerant of a competitor is doomed, and any business comfortable with being second will end up being last!"[3] This thinking is very much a part of the culture of Oracle.

Kill or Be Killed

Larry Ellison's strategy of attacking Oracle's competitors has a single goal: the demise of that business. It is kill or be killed as companies in the industry—established firms and upstarts—fight for market share. That Oracle has won many of the battles it has waged is impressive when one considers the number of organizations in competition with it. If you consider Oracle's competitors by product type, there are

> **Larry Ellison's strategy of attacking Oracle's competitors has a single goal: the demise of that business.**

Sybase, Inc., Informix Corp. (now IBM), Computer Associates International, Progress Software Corp., Software AG, Microsoft Corp., and IBM Corp., all competitors in development of database management systems. Microsoft and Sybase are also on the list of application development and business tool developers. Add Forte Software (now part of Sun Microsystems, Inc.), Business Objects SA, and Cognos, Inc. Finally, among client-service business application developers, Oracle has faced down SAP AG, PeopleSoft, Inc., and Baan Company.

Targeting Competitors

What does this mean in business terms? Oracle picks its business targets and then develops its marketing campaign against each one to get the upper hand. Stuart Read, a seven-year veteran of Oracle where he was a senior director of the New Media Group, director of network products, and group product manager, described its tactics against a number of companies in his book *The Oracle Edge*. I spoke with Mark Jarvis, senior vice president of marketing for Oracle, during the course of writing this book to confirm that the company hasn't changed those tactics. Oracle completes a detailed study of the competitor's organization and product line. Once it has completed its evaluation and has identified every shortcoming, it writes and distributes its findings to its sales force. Subsequent marketing plays up the competitor's shortcomings. The hero in those old war and Western movies I watch late into the night would describe the tactic as "fighting on the hero's terms."

A campaign is built that defines the competitor in a manner that enables sales representatives to subtly—and sometimes not so subtly—put down a competitor's products. The campaigns themselves are waged in industry and business magazines, during sales calls to prospective customers, and in Silicon Valley on billboards that line Route 101. When Oracle buys ads in periodicals, they are strategically placed—right hand page, front of the magazine. The ads themselves point out what a competitor's products can't do and either directly or indirectly raise this question to the chief information officers (CIOs) reading them: "Why bet your career on a product like that?"

Although Ellison is very much known today for his involvement in product development, he has always played a key role in the organization's marketing, according to Jarvis. In the firm's early beginnings (see Chapter 1), while cofounders Edward Oates and Bob Miner focused on product development, it was Ellison who spearheaded Oracle's marketing efforts, which may explain the use of aggressive campaigns since the company's launch.

Their effectiveness, too, may be attributed to Ellison, who not only knows his company's strengths and weaknesses but those issues about database purchase that concern customers: performance, cost, the number and kinds of platforms and applications, vendor knowledge of customer needs, reliability, vendor support, and ease of use.

> **Giant copies of Oracle ads, in which bar charts compare Oracle's sales performance to that of the competition, hang in office corridors.**

Naturally, when Oracle launches a campaign, that campaign plays up its strengths and its competitors' weaknesses. Often, Oracle ads employ what the firm calls "functional marketing"—that is, features and benefits comparisons and performance numbers that compare Oracle performance against statistics on the competition's products. These comparative advertisements are effective because Oracle has a clear and accurate idea about those factors that influence prospective clients.

This understanding isn't limited to what customers want the products to do. Based on focus groups, Ellison and his team also know the kinds of advertisements that CIOs look at, the magazines they purchase, and the worth of benchmark data to them in making a decision. Benchmark charts are central to the company's marketing campaigns. CIOs use the data in these ads to better prepare to make the costly decisions about which product to purchase.

At Oracle headquarters, staff members are kept apprised of all ad campaigns. Giant copies of Oracle ads, in which bar charts compare Oracle's sales performance to that of the competition, hang in office corridors.

Gloves-Off Campaigns: From Sharks to Crib Death

Advertising campaigns from Oracle have been described as "in your face," tough challenges to competitors. Take Oracle's long-term campaign with Informix Database Assets, a campaign that is likely to continue since its acquisition by IBM, the newest and biggest contender for Oracle's 50 percent market share of the database management market.

Competition with Informix began in the mid-1980s. Informix was a contender for market leader, and Oracle had no intention of giving up ground to the firm with its data management product portfolio. Aware that a picture is worth a thousand words, Oracle came up with a great graphic that it used in ads and even put on T-shirts that were given to prospective customers. The graphic was of an old-style diver on the bottom of the ocean with Informix written on his chest. The line carrying air to the diver was in the mouth of a shark swimming above him. On the shark was the word "Oracle."

The battle with Informix even went beyond ads. For example, Oracle raided Informix personnel. Shocked? You shouldn't be. Wal-Mart's Sam Walton, in his book *Made in America: My Story*, admitted to the same practice as he visited competitors' stores, recruiting top sales personnel. During the early years at Amazon.com, Jeff Bezos recruited from Wal-Mart to get expertise about its distribution system. That it is accepted practice doesn't stop a firm from suing, which is what Informix did. Oracle responded with a billboard in Silicon Valley ridiculing the Informix lawsuit against the thirteen engineers who had defected to Oracle. The sign read: INFORMIX: HIRING LAWYERS EXPERIENCED IN SUING PROGRAMMERS. ORACLE: HIRING EXPERIENCED PROGRAMMERS.

When it came to Informix, Oracle didn't limit its raids to sales folk and other employees, a practice that by itself increased Oracle's knowledge of Informix products and decreased both the morale and number of its competitor's employees. Oracle also approached producers of software that made up Informix's portfolio and convinced them about the merits of being associated with the top company in the field, not the second best firm. Oracle even took a poke at Informix's leadership at the time. After unearthing a copy of then-president Philip White's travel schedule, Oracle launched its "Where is Phil White?" campaign, sending an Oracle sales team wherever White went.

To send the message that Informix was not an industry leader, Oracle came up with a slogan that reflected its opinion of Informix's database development efforts: "Always a bridesmaid, never a bride." Whether Informix's product development compared well to Oracle's or not, the marketing offensive worked successfully with information officers of Fortune 500 firms whose mind-set was to purchase the premium product.

Before you feel sorry for Informix, let me share with you another Silicon Valley story that suggests the managers at Informix got theirs back. In 1996, as Oracle was overcoming its 1990 financial crisis and the tight Asian market, Informix

> To send the message that Informix was not an industry leader, Oracle came up with a slogan about Informix's database development: "Always a bridesmaid, never a bride."

posted an ad on a billboard it had purchased several years before along Route 101 near the Oracle exit. On one occasion, the billboard had a picture of Oracle headquarters with a yellow sign: WARNING: DINOSAUR CROSSING. Another time, a billboard had a picture of Ellison with devil's horns growing from his head.

This might have been retaliation for an ad that Oracle had placed on a "traveling billboard" that it drove into Informix's parking lot. The text read, "Gentlemen, start your snails," and the graphic benchmarked Oracle against Informix with Oracle numbers highlighted in red and Informix numbers resembling snail trails. Likewise, its competitor's logo was redesigned to resemble a snail.

Don't believe that a slogan or, in Oracle's case, a label can influence customers? Heard enough times, such messages will stick and significantly affect competitors' sales. Unless a company reacts immediately, it could be pigeonholed. In another campaign, Oracle did in a database company founded by professors from the University of California, Berkeley that was heavily staffed with recent graduates. The firm, Ingres, may have offered better technology than Oracle, but Oracle succeeded in killing the firm by labeling its effort "The Research Project." Not only did Oracle effectively kill a potentially tough competitor, it hired away some talented engineers. Recruiters from Oracle waited outside with employment applications as the engineers walked away from their offices in 1994. In its campaign against another competitor, Sybase, Oracle came up with buttons that sales reps wore on which were the words "Sybase: Crib Death." So Oracle planted the suggestion in potential customers' minds that the newly formed database management system

(DBMS) developer wouldn't succeed. Noting that Sybase offered a product that had to be combined with partner tools and applications, Oracle literature referred to the firm as "the Erector set company." Oracle sales reps would ask

> Sybase offered a product that had to be combined with partner tools and applications, so Oracle literature referred to the firm as "the Erector set company."

potential Sybase customers, "Who will you call when you have a problem?"[4] Sybase saw itself as an innovator, leading the industry in its approach to database management system development, so initially it welcomed its competitor's jabs. As it began to lose sales to Oracle, it tried to change its image, even acquired two firms, Gains and Powersoft, to offer its own package. But it was too late.

The Battles Wage On

When Oracle chose to adapt its database to run on a PC platform, it didn't change its marketing tactics at all. One of the first companies it attacked was Ashton-Tate (which was later acquired by Borland Software Corp.). Its dBASE relational DBMS was the most popular offering, but it could run only on a PC platform and could not support a number of users. Consequently, Oracle labeled it a "toy" unsuitable for use in a business environment. Cullinet Software, Inc., another producer of a dBASE program, was a mature company, but Oracle's sales representatives repeatedly referred to it as "old" when they visited Fortune 500 firms that wanted the latest products in the field. (Cullinet is now a part of Computer Associates.)

Of course, as Oracle moved to develop portable database software—that is, database software that could run on any PC—it was inevitable that it would find itself competing with the likes of IBM Corp., Hewlett-Packard Co., Digital Equipment Corp., and other producers of database software suitable only for use on their proprietary hardware.

Once again, Oracle management and employees went into a huddle to acquire all the information they could on the competition. The logical sales approach Ellison and his management team decided for Oracle was to remind prospects that the nature of computers was changing rapidly. If a company wanted the flexibility that would enable it to purchase the fastest, cheapest model, it needed to purchase software that would work on any computer—in other words, Oracle's.

Digital Computer Equipment (DEC) tried to win back market share lost to Oracle by offering its relational product, RDB, free to its customers. Before DEC made its announcement, Oracle learned about the offer and countered with an ad that said, "Even if RDB Were Free, You Couldn't Afford It." When Oracle demonstrated that it could sell its product while DEC gave its away, Digital gave in, selling its RDB database software operation to Oracle in 1994.

Clearly, Ellison has built Oracle's reputation as a tough competitor. If you put aside issues of personality that admittedly swirl about Ellison (and I suspect that he enjoys), he and his management team do no more than any other senior management would do to compete successfully against their competitors. For one, they track the industry carefully to identify (1) upstarts with the potential to steal market share, (2) mature companies with vulnerabilities that could position them to take customers from them, and (3) business opportunities not yet fully recognized by a company with no more than a toehold in the market.

Not impressed? This tactic isn't so unlike that of traditional product positioning. But consider this in the context of the digital world, where a month is equivalent to a year for traditional operations. Victory is truly to the swiftest—to those who reposition to changes in either competitors' products or customer needs or both, not to mention your own product line. To compete under such conditions, the mantra "crush the competition" isn't solely a marketing slogan but an assessment of a product's benefits.

For instance, in Oracle's campaign against Ingres, it didn't only label the youthful company of recent graduates as a "Research Project"; it also did a benefit-by-benefit comparison of its relational technology and that of Ingres. After identifying those elements that were critical to a relational database and creating a chart that compared the strengths of Oracle's product against those of Ingres's technology, Oracle created advertisements that played up its capabilities and played down those of Ingres. Ingres's engineers, however, were good, and they were able to fix the real deficiencies noted by Oracle in its ad campaigns. A change in market positioning was needed on Oracle's part. What did Ellison do?

Analysis of the situation disclosed that Ingres, in satisfying some customer needs, had created a problem for itself: Data processing was slow. This was not a problem at Oracle. New ads began to appear comparing the two firms' delivery of

> The mantra "crush the competition" isn't solely a marketing slogan but an assessment of a product's benefits.

databases. The rivalry didn't end there. Ingres soon caught up with Oracle in terms of performance, which meant another shift in positioning on Oracle's part. Ellison looked at the business horizon and realized that Ingres's product worked on fewer platforms than Oracle software did. So Oracle created a new comparison chart that listed all the computers on which Oracle software worked. Although Ingres toiled to make its software more portable, it was too late. Within a year, the firm folded.

Is Ellison the bad boy of Silicon Valley? No, he's simply a good CEO with an understanding of the parameters corporate customers use to compare database software.

The Battle with Microsoft

If you look through the press clippings about Larry Ellison's jousting with Bill Gates, the press clearly has benefited the most from the competition of these two computer giants and the organizations they lead.

Despite his laid-back manner and nerdy appearance in comparison to Ellison's hyper behavior and dapper dress, Gates has an ego as large as Ellison's—and to Ellison's chagrin, there are more pictures of Gates on the covers of business magazines to support his image as the software industry's biggest celebrity. David Kaplan tells a Silicon Valley story about a *Fortune* magazine interview done with Andy Grove, chairman of Intel, during which Grove was asked who had inspired him. He replied, "Steve Jobs." Grove went on to point to the Apple founder's career, which has gone from PC to Pixar, his computer-animated movie and game company. When Gates read the article, so the story goes, he called Grove. "What about *all that I've done?*" he protested.[5]

Roger Bamford, one of Oracle's chief software programmers, told Kaplan, "Oracle may be the second-largest software company, but for Larry that's the kiss of death. Being number two drives Larry crazy."[6] And Gates is number one.

Kaplan attributes the conflict between the two men to what he labels "the dueling of the IPOs."[7] Oracle went public on March 12, 1986, one day ahead of Microsoft. After Oracle's initial public offering, Ellison's worth was $93.5 million. The following day, when Microsoft went public, however, Gates found his worth was more than three times that of Ellison—$300 million. The Microsoft story pushed Oracle off the news pages.

IBM's Negligence

The two firms crossed paths before their IPO moment. Both companies came into being due to the negligence of the same firm: IBM Corp. In 1976, engineers at the IBM Research Laboratory wrote a paper describing a database system that would allow customers to store and find the correct data with a few simple questions. However, this relational model was only a model, a paper version of how a relational database system would work. This paper model was published by IBM in the belief that doing so was good PR, supporting IBM's reputation as the standard setter in the high-tech field. IBM released its research to the technology community because 1) it supported the image of IBM as the alpha dog in a high-tech pack and 2) it erred in not recognizing the commercial value of its findings.

At Oracle, however, Oates became fascinated with the concept. But it was Ellison who saw how IBM's discovery could legitimize his fledgling's firm's offer of relational software. Furthermore, if his firm could beat Big Blue to the market with the software, they would have it made.

IBM later did recognize the commercial value, and it began to develop a language for it in 1980. In 1982, the same engineers at IBM created a command language—the

Structured Query Language (SQL)—based on plain English that would allow anyone with typing skill to access the data. But it was too late. By then, the Ellison group, which capitalized on the commercial application of the idea and borrowed it, had already been marketing its own database software for five years.

In the case of Microsoft, in 1980, IBM signed a deal with Microsoft that made Microsoft's MS-DOS operating system the preferred one for IBM's first PC. More critical, the agreement allowed Microsoft to license that operating system to any hardware manufacturer. From this blunder emerged the Microsoft/Intel computer, a commodity-like computer that anyone could assemble, and the likes of Dell and Compaq.

Personality Conflict

If you think of the personalities of Gates and Ellison and the tracks their organizations are on, it is inevitable that they would lock horns—time and time and time again. And the stories do make good press, no matter which camp you are in. For the record, though, despite his reputation as a ruthless competitor, Ellison has his followers, just as Gates does. Paul R. LaMonica, writing for *Red Herring*, said, "My heart goes out to him. . . . One would think that Mr. Ellison was not simply a software company executive but actually a person to hide your children from." He continued, "The market obsesses with Mr. Ellison's personality quirks; it ignores the fact that Oracle is a fantastic company."[8] He went on to suggest that the company itself, too, was a victim of the market's unreasonable expectations.

Since Microsoft and Oracle went public, Oracle's leader has had differences of opinion with Microsoft's leader. Take, for example, the very public discussion on the future of the

> It was inevitable that Ellison and Gates would lock horns—time and time and time again.

PC at the European Information Technology Forum in Paris (see Chapter 7). Ellison's proposed network appliances—pared-down computers without hard drives or traditional desktop operating systems—would level the playing field, making room in the marketplace not only for Oracle but Sun Microsystems's open programming system called Java and Netscape Communications' Internet browser. The problem was that until then, Oracle had done nothing to create or market the product. Kaplan calls it typical Ellison: "Talk first, execute later."[9]

By 2000, as Ellison had predicted, there were cheap desktop computers linked to the Internet. But the computers were traditional Windows-based PCs, not network appliances. Ellison hyperbole notwithstanding, Gates had seen the ramifications *and* marketing value in the idea, and with Microsoft's faster development capability and solid reputation in the marketplace, his firm was able to adapt Ellison's idea with significant bottom-line benefit. Likewise, Microsoft seized on another Ellison idea—a network computer that links the Internet to a television set—when it launched WebTV.

As Ellison attempts to make Oracle the software producer of choice for e-businesses, he also has to fight off incursions from Gates's "stripped down" Microsoft into the same business.

As e-enabling information has become critical to doing business in the New Economy, the two software behemoths are competing for the evolving marketplace. When it comes to pricing, Microsoft has the edge. Oracle will have to make substantial cuts to compete in the lower-end market. Price isn't an issue at the higher end of the market, however, where

> **As Ellison attempts to make Oracle the software producer of choice for e-businesses, he has to fight off incursions from Gates's "stripped down" Microsoft into the same business.**

the quality of products and security of the data are more important to corporate customers. Technicians have said that Oracle's support for multiple platforms means it is easier to integrate into an organization's existing infrastructure. The SQL Server, as with most Microsoft products, has been written and optimized to run on Windows, which means that Microsoft not only has to persuade users that SQL Servers are the best option, but also to purchase Windows 2000. Ellison has questioned the speed at which data can be run on a Microsoft server, because it uses Windows.

Microsoft's response came at an industry conference in January 2001. Mugs that were distributed to conference attendees poked fun at Ellison's offer to give customers $1 million if they couldn't run Oracle 9i database software three times faster than competing products from IBM and Microsoft, suggesting such an offer was a sales ploy. The promotion said, "When an Oracle salesman pitches $5 million of overpriced software, simply glance at the [Microsoft] mug. Oracle salesman spots mug, offers 10 percent discount," said the Microsoft promotion.

Clearly, there is significant competition between Ellison and Gates and Oracle and Microsoft, and occasionally it's personal. But Ellison and Gates, egos aside, are just playing the game in the tech field—the business game.

IBM Enters the Picture

Incidentally, as you monitor Oracle's competition, keep your eye not only on upstarts—there are new players daily—but old-timers. Old-timers like IBM, which has begun to compete with Oracle and Microsoft for the number-one spot in the corporate software world. IBM has acquired Informix's enterprise database assets. At the time of the acquisition, IBM said, "IBM and Informix are impressive as separate entities, and together the newly formed data management team will continue to deliver the most innovative technologies at the best value to customers." Janet Perna, general manager for IBM Data Management Solutions, went on to promise, "IBM is focused on setting the standard for the next-generation e-business solutions."[10]

This battle of the titans is difficult to call—even if you eliminate Microsoft from the equation.

While Oracle offers customers a complete and tightly integrated package of software—everything a company needs to manage its numbers, manufacturing, sales force, e-commerce transactions, and supply chain—IBM has quilted together a package of business software from various companies, including itself. If IBM succeeds, it will win a larger portion of the $50 billion corporate software market, but it will also make room for major application providers such as SAP, Siebel (whose founder and CEO, incidentally, came from Oracle), PeopleSoft, and others. If Oracle wins, it will be pushing its own applications. According to investors, IBM has found a key Oracle vulnerability: Oracle competes in the applications market with the same software makers it relies on to help sell its databases. Since IBM doesn't sell applications of its own, it is hoping these firms will recommend IBM to customers rather than Oracle.

How likely is it that IBM will beat Oracle at its own game? In the late 1980s, as business applications software companies were launched, they built their software to run on Oracle's database, even though Oracle also sold its own competing applications software. Analysts suggested in the mid-1990s that those software companies helped drive at least 25 percent of Oracle's database sales. As Ellison focuses on e-businesses,

> **Don't overlook the fact that "old timer" IBM continues to be a viable contender in this market.**

database sales have stagnated whereas IBM sales are surging. Analysts are unsure, but they do expect IBM and Oracle will be among the strongest players in the market.

If you wonder what Ellison has planned to address this challenge, just visit Oracle Corp.'s Web site and read "Ten Questions IBM Doesn't Want You to Ask About Portals." (If Oracle follows its usual marketing practices, you can also get a copy of this document from your Oracle sales rep.) With his disdain for the idea of corporations buying and hooking together major software components from different suppliers, Ellison already has offered this critique of IBM's database management effort: "You would never buy a car that way."[11]

Management Analysis

Oracle is ruthless in competing with other software companies. If it weren't, it would easily have been overshadowed by bigger firms when it was young. If it squeaked by, it would be in a very niched market, not at all the size business it is today.

What about this Gates/Ellison competition? Why not? It has made Oracle as much a household name as Microsoft—and that was its purpose. Keep in mind that when Ellison first met Gates, he admired him. But business is business. If Microsoft, IBM, SAP—you name it—gets in the way of Oracle, Ellison can be expected—should be expected—to go for the jugular.

LOCKING IN CLIENTS FOR LIFE

sales and service support

In the customer-centric culture that
organizations boast of today, Larry Ellison may be one of the
few executives who has been known to use the F-word when
referring to his customers—even talking to them. It is not
from disdain but from frustration—frustration that they don't
appreciate the solution he and his firm is offering. Besides, it
is part of the "bad boy" attitude that others in the high-tech
industry say he works so hard to promote. After all, it gets
Oracle in the press, a not-so-small achievement when one
thinks about how many firms are out there competing for the
attention of the press as well as users.

Larry as Top Salesman

From the beginning, given his high visibility, Ellison has

been Oracle's top salesman. When the company was first launched, Ellison had the job of convincing chief information and accounting officers and information technology (IT) personnel, first, that there was a need for a product like the one his firm had developed—relational databases—and then, second, that they should buy that product from Oracle. As soon as Oracle had identified the commercial value of relational data management, other firms quickly entered the market created for them by Oracle and its top spokesperson. Ellison spent those first few years as head of Oracle going from one industry meeting after another extolling the worth of relational programs.

Oracle sustained its dominant market position. After all, Oracle's systems allowed users not only to key in data on their own and, using standard language, massage that data and create useful management reports, but also to switch computer platforms if they so decided (although there might be a fee to do so). It was a compelling selling point to prospective buyers, thereby making Oracle the market leader.

From the subsequent competition came a mantra that still drives Oracle: "Lock in the customers, lock out competitors." In short, Oracle is focused on building clients for life. Indeed, it has lifted customer retention to an art form. What does Oracle do?

Part of the answer is tied to the products themselves. On the simplest level, choice of a database system is a costly decision that is unlikely to be reconsidered once made. The difficulty associated with implementation of a relational database also makes it difficult for a competitor to move in and take over an existing account. Not only must a customer buy the competitive product and pay charges for

> **An Oracle mantra: "Lock in the customers, lock out competitors."**

entering the data, since export of the data from one system to another is often impossible, but the customer must also build applications using the competitive product and learn how to use that product. Consequently, there can be a long learning curve.

Equally important, Oracle sets its sights high, focusing its sales efforts on the chief information officer (CIO) or higher-level executive and thereafter establishing a strategic relationship with the customer. These high-profile customers are referred to as "points of pressure," or POPs, executives caught in a triad of information overload, corporate strategy (including Web presence), and tactics (which today encompass Web-enabled applications as well as database management).[1] Building a sales force that can approach these senior executives is one reason behind the three-piece-suit image that drives Oracle's culture; only a polished sales professional with a Rolodex can call on senior officers, carry out a slick product demonstration, and talk strategy, not technology, to these executives.

In short, Oracle hires "executives" who can talk to potential customers' executives. These are, after all, the individuals who can sign off on the high cost of an enterprise database solution. Furthermore, once an Oracle sales professional has made a sale at this level, it is more likely to generate more sales than a competitor selling a software program to someone at a much lower level in the organization can. After the sale, Oracle can expect internal support from the POP's IT staff.

You can almost say that sales to a point of pressure for Oracle makes it the standard database provider for that POP's organization.

These customers can commit to a trial license to evaluate Oracle software for a thirty-day period—"lock in the customers"—or a perpetual license that has no time limit unless terminated following the process set in the contract— "lock out the competitors." The organization also offers two- and four-year term licenses, but at about one-third and two-thirds, respectively, of the cost of perpetual licenses, thereby making it more cost-effective for a customer to select a perpetual license and for Oracle to effectively "lock out competition."

Making Contact

Oracle has even created events to enable its regional sales folk to make contact with prospective customers. In its Redwood Shores campus, for example, Oracle has a briefing center used primarily for day-long events that spotlight the newest in

Oracle technology. When there, businesspeople are treated first-class—at Oracle, what else would you expect? Potential customers also have the opportunity to meet the company's

> "The Excitement Factor" is used at customer relationship-building meetings to generate interest in upcoming products or new applications of existing ones.

executive management, including Larry Ellison himself. Once a year, Oracle also brings together customers and prospects for a worldwide conference where product marketing managers and Oracle developers talk face-to-face with customers, and vice versa. Customers can also network with one another, and these conversations often trigger new ideas for applications. Ellison keynotes the event with exciting predictions about the future. That's where he assumes his Barnum persona with his humbug (think "rosy possibilities").

Both within and outside Oracle this is what has been labeled "The Excitement Factor." Turning a mundane issue on its head can stimulate thinking that in turn leads to an exciting opportunity at Oracle. The Excitement Factor is also used at these customer relationship-building meetings to generate interest in upcoming products or new applications of existing ones.

Clearly, whether we are talking about one-on-one meetings or full-day conferences with banquets, the events have one thing in common. It is Oracle's belief in the need to remain in communications with customers to ensure a lasting relationship with them. I'm not just referring to members of its sales force. Opportunities are found for development personnel to speak with customers to better understand their business needs and, maybe more important, truly appreciate their frustrations when a system doesn't work as promised.

Oracle has also facilitated the creation of independent, global user groups that offer a means to learn about Oracle products and exchange ideas with other Oracle users, from traditional database programs to its applications programs. There are live meetings for which Oracle provides funding,

> **To purchase a product from Oracle is to be a member of a very special club.**

speakers, and meeting support; there are also online user group meetings through the corporate Web site *(www.oracle.com)* so visitors can participate. Oracle also maintains regular audio- and videocasts from its site.

To purchase a product from Oracle is to be a member of a very special club, which is why Oracle also created its own membership program. Club Oracle brings people together both to discuss Oracle products and to network. From that networking, members can explore opportunities for their individual businesses (though these opportunities are, the cynic in me suggests, most likely tied to an Oracle product).

These are not Oracle's only initiatives, however. The company also offers services to make it easier for prospective customers to do business with it and other programs designed to support existing customers' programs. Many of these programs are a reflection of Oracle's e-business focus.

Crushing That Competition

Chapter 4 addressed another Oracle mantra attributed to Ellison: "Crush the competition." This directive is related to customer service. After all, every customer that Oracle lost would be a customer another firm would win. Consequently, Oracle wants to minimize the likelihood of losing customers by minimizing the number of competitors out there (think of the behavior of a stallion toward another stallion trying to cut mares from the herd, or a queen bee killing off nascent queens to keep the beehive to herself). Take this concept further in terms of sales and customer relationship building, and it becomes evident that once you win a customer, you want that business as your customer forever.

Initially, it was Oracle's engineering strengths that made the sales for the fledgling company, but it was its expertise with the technology that locked competitors out.

Market Leadership

The database software that were the foundation of Oracle's initial growth required expert engineering talent and little customer relationship building. Despite some shortcomings in those early systems, the systems sold themselves. Ellison aimed for 100 percent growth, and to achieve that growth he doubled the size of his sales force annually. In those early years, there were supposedly no carefully considered sales projections as there are today. Rather, Ellison hired the most competitive sales folks he could find and kept the best sales-people motivated with big bonuses. If you could take a cus-tomer from one of the competitors targeted to be crushed by the organization, you got a bigger commission. Those sale professionals who couldn't hack it were let go. It was a sim-ple proposition. Go in, sell your product, and get out. There was no effort to build a relationship with customers or to practice relationship marketing. When problems arose with those early systems, however, those early customers could get access to not only Robert Miner and Ed Oates, the two pro-grammers who created the first software, but Ellison as well.

Although Oracle was the market leader, its quality reputa-tion wasn't that good during the early years. However, repu-tation didn't seem to matter to customers who were willing to accept the foibles of the company to get their hands on the newest, latest, next big thing for sale. Marketing experts tell me that this is typical customer behavior during creation of a market, which was very much the case during Oracle's early years. Ellison wasn't selling the largest elephant or smallest man in the world, but like Barnum, whose audience was open to exciting new things, his audience of IT managers were receptive to his promises.

Decentralized Sales Support

As Oracle grew, it provided customer support through field sales offices throughout the United States and abroad. By providing a number of field support engineers in each office with sales personnel, Oracle could ensure that customers could readily reach help when the need arose. These support engineers were expected to keep sales personnel in touch with client firms long after a contract was signed. In particular, using feedback from customer support, the sales representatives knew when to make another sales call to sell other Oracle programs or upgrades of the original program.

These customer support engineers were expected to know their stuff, of course. There are bugs revealed during implementation of any program, and as bugs and other difficulties were exposed, the field support engineers were taught how to fix them. Readily accessible sales reps and engineering support locked out competitors by ensuring customers that they could pick up a phone and call to have support in the office within a few hours if need be. They also locked in customers with leading-edge, sophisticated technology and regular upgrades in response to customer responses.

Centralized Selling

Much has changed since those first years, not only for Oracle, but for the entire software industry as well. The marketplace is much more sophisticated; Oracle has stronger competitors than ever before, although it is correct to say that at least two-thirds of the Fortune 100 companies use Oracle software somewhere in their organizations and that Oracle is the second-largest software company in the world. Market sophistication, in itself, has meant changes in how Oracle sells and supports customers. Oracle may continue to promote an entrepreneurial culture, but because of its size it is a mature business today, and this, too, has led to changes.

For one, Oracle now has a powerful telephone sales force that is regionally organized. Furthermore, customer support is now centralized and responsible for selling upgrades and maintenance contracts. Support is handled via the Web as well as through a traditional call center. Oracle created profit centers to handle education and consulting, thereby further focusing field sales force attention away from account management and into new business. Revenue today comes from sales and services, and services include maintenance, consulting, and education.

Any discussion of sales and customer support must make mention of the most important development at Oracle today; that is, the expansion beyond its core database programs into its e-business suite of business applications that range from customer relationship management (CRM) to human relations management to inventory control to manufacturing. Oracle has moved onto the Internet, which has meant that applications and customer support can be provided via the Web (think Dell). To date, Oracle has provided its integrated E-Business Suite of business applications as a fully managed and supported online service to more than 125 customers worldwide. Consequently, Oracle's long-term goal—no downtime—has become even more important, as has an understanding of its customers' business needs, from the Fortune 100 to businesses with fewer than a hundred employees.

Oracle sales are built on a clear understanding of its customers' businesses, relationship marketing, and thorough customer support. Although this formula is almost a decade old, its practice remains essential to the firm as it moves aggressively into the applications field. After all, about one tenth of Oracle's sales would be endangered. When Oracle tells potential customers on Oracle.com that "with the power behind our online business services, you remove the complexity of managing your applications and can focus on your

> **Oracle sales are built on a clear understanding of customers' businesses, relationship marketing, and thorough customer support.**

core business," it is making a major commitment to prospective customers. It is a commitment that requires a true appreciation of customers' needs and the capability to support their systems thereafter. All this brings us back to sustaining trust and deepening the customer relationship. After all, the firmer Oracle's relationship with an existing client, the more likely it will win a new project from that same customer without a lot of competition—and the greater the chances that it can aggressively price the service.

E-Consulting

In the software industry, trustworthiness is a major factor in winning customers. An IT professional told me, "The software services business is a people business, and nothing sells a company better than the quality of its people."[2] He was referring to a firm's consulting contingent. Just as Oracle has assembled a top-caliber sales force, it's also assembled experienced consultants to spearhead systems programs or work with IT staff to move such programs through. Over the years, these individuals have developed solid reputations in the industry.

In 1999, however, Oracle significantly changed its consulting service, offering "e-consulting" as well as traditional consulting services. "Integrated software, like the Oracle E-Business Suite, paves the way for a new world order of implementation," said Sandy Sanderson, executive vice president for Oracle. "The stage is set for the potential demise of the traditional software services business because of the tremendous costs associated with the antiquated methods of working to interface disparate applications."[3] To support its e-consulting service, Oracle has 12,500 consulting experts in fifty countries. There is even round-the-clock implementation with teams expertly and efficiently addressing repeatable, fixed-scope deliverables. From the day a prospective customer orders the Oracle E-Business Suite via the Oracle Store on its Web site to the time the customer's business can go live with a new application, it may be only ninety days or less. Valerie Borthwick, senior vice president of Oracle's Global Consulting Services and Solutions, observes: "We continue to seek new

> **To support its e-consulting, Oracle has 12,500 consulting experts in 50 countries.**

ways of delivering services, both in terms of prepackaging of common services as well as the use of leading methods of delivery—all of this driving more choices and lower costs for our customers." As legacy firms seek a Web presence, they are searching for experienced solution providers. "By choosing Oracle e-consulting," says Borthwick, "customers have direct access to the expertise accumulated by Oracle itself in the process of transforming its own business to the Web."[4]

A visit to Oracle.com can be overwhelming because you are bombarded with the myriad services beyond e-consulting that are available from Oracle. From the moment Larry Ellison determined to grow Oracle beyond its database boundaries to support the transformation of increasing numbers of companies to click-and-brick businesses, the Web site has become central to the company as a vehicle for delivering software and services. When you visit the site, you can purchase anything you need to solve your company's need for software products, services, support, and education.

For example, customers with Oracle support contracts can access Oracle MetaLink from the Web site to request technical assistance, receive proactive customized support alerts, and other information tailored to their specific needs. MetaLink service allows Oracle to track recurring problems in a system and alert customers before problem occurrence in order to help customers remedy their systems problems. The site allows customer to post and view questions and answers, download solutions, access product lifecycle information (including upcoming upgrades), and conduct a knowledge-

> **Support services have been redesigned to align with the "every second counts" operational needs of e-business customers.**

base search. Data about customer problems collected by Oracle from this site are also shared with program developers as they work on new offerings.

At one time, Oracle offered three kinds of support services. Bronze service provided 9 A.M. to 5 P.M. service support; Silver extended that support beyond work hours; and Gold service offered 24/7 support, all based on price paid. Today, as a consequence of Oracle's own conversion to a 100 percent e-business, support services have been redesigned to align with the "every second counts" operational needs of e-business customers. In addition to MetaLink, customers can purchase premium support that includes direct access to Oracle's technical analysts via the Web or telephone. Technical analysts serve as advisers, coaches, cheerleaders, and teachers.

The Educational Side of Oracle

If there is one element that locks out competitors, it is the education services that Oracle offers not only its own talented employees but its customers. When you become an Oracle customer, you get a license of some duration that covers use of the software, technical support, and access to Oracle University.

Founded in 1999, Oracle University enrolls more than 500,000 students annually. There are 750 instructors and 400 different courses. A key component of Oracle's services, the university has a total staff of a little over 2,500 employees in almost 150 countries. Jeremy Burton, senior vice president of product marketing, explained the purpose in combining the disparate parts of the company that provided courses and educational materials: "Oracle University cultivates the skilled professionals who will grow the Oracle Economy." In other words, if Oracle is to lock customers in and lock out competitors, it needs to "get more skilled Oracle people into the marketplace."

Ellison has called education a core competency of Oracle. John Hall, senior vice president of Oracle University, recalled a meeting with Ellison immediately after formation of the organization. From the conversation, it was evident that Ellison believed that no one could do a better job of providing support and education on Oracle products than Oracle itself. In accelerating the adoption of Oracle technology, education in general and Oracle University per se are strategic businesses for the enterprise. To ensure a close relationship between Oracle the company and Oracle the university, those who work on curriculum are also part of product groups. The more advanced their knowledge of new programs, the better able they would be to write education materials—and earlier in the product cycle as well.

By the year 2003, Oracle expects its university to bring in almost $1 billion from classroom sessions and another $200 million from online services. However, Oracle University isn't the only way that Ellison and his management team are pursuing education as a direct, as well as indirect, profit center. Only a few months after founding Oracle University, the company announced its Oracle Learning Network (OLN), a subscription-based online education resource. The program

> **Ellison has called education a "core competency of Oracle." More than 500,000 students enroll in Oracle University annually.**

uploads four to six hours of new educational content to OLN weekly for subscribers or students who pay $1,500 per year for unlimited access to the site. Nowhere but in the high-tech field is continuing learning a lifelong objective, and OLN acts as continuing education for those who have completed Oracle's certification process.

There is yet another reason for the emphasis on education, aside from making customers skilled in use of Oracle technology and, indirectly, committing IT personnel who have devoted hours to training to continue to use Oracle product. The more skilled the users of Oracle technology are, the less technical support they need, and that's an economic savings for Oracle.

Management Analysis

Oracle's model of sales/customer support clearly is worth consideration, and not only for high-tech companies. It can be adapted by other companies from manufacturers to service providers as they move their businesses onto the Web.

Lock in customers, lock out competitors. It seems a simple directive but it is far from an easy one, for any company. For a software firm, it would seem doubly difficult, given the competition within the industry. By raising it to a corporate value, and tying corporate behaviors to it, however, Ellison gave the words substance.

But there are reasons beyond this to explain why Oracle clients stick with the software firm: Oracle products are on the cutting edge and the firm has a customer-centric attitude. A software firm isn't one of the largest in the industry simply because its sales folk wear three-piece suits.

PRODUCT DEVELOPMENT
looking beyond today

enough books to fill an eight-foot-high bookcase with books left over. And one little typo, or a bug in a single line of code, could cause the entire system to crash. Actually 100 percent of a software program has to be accurate to work "kinda okay."

The fact that Oracle has divided its product development operation into two groups—one that continues to focus on its flagship product (i.e., Oracle 8i database) and another to focus

> **Actually 100 percent of a software program has to be accurate to work "kinda okay."**

on its applications products (i.e., Oracle 11i)—is only the surface story of how Oracle approaches software development. To understand the reasons for its success, however, it is important also to understand the factors that need to be managed. You will then be better able to appreciate the strategic imperatives that drive Oracle's product development.

The Obstacles in Software Development

Let's begin with recognition that software programs of the size that Oracle develops are as complex as drawing a blueprint for a bridge on shifting sands. Then there are additional complicating factors. Let's go through some of them.

You aren't absolutely sure where your customer wants the bridge built. In the software industry, customer needs aren't always easy to identify. Needs evolve, and frequently architecture can't be completed to allow for later changes. Otherwise, work would have to be redone—expensive work for the company to absorb.

You may have to expand the bridge after the first wagon goes over it. Already the software requirements are vague, but add to that the fact that the design must allow for a broad range of needs and also be extendable for later upgrades, which are often a necessity in the field as one competitor releases a me-too program that must be surpassed.

You may think you have the requirements set and can proceed, and then they change. Yahoo! had to rework its My Yahoo! personalized Web site three times before its launch in 1997 just to reflect features that competitors had added to their sites since the start of work.

You suddenly discover design flaws. These flaws weren't evident when you began, but suddenly you discover a glitch that you could not have anticipated as being a problem. In our bridge analogy, you may suddenly discover you have included bridge spans of a metal that won't stand up to traffic at capacity once roads are built on both sides of the bridge. You have to rethink your original costs, redo your schedule, and maybe redesign the bridge. In the software industry, you may determine that you incorporated a design element meant to speed the process itself, but during early tests you discover that the element does more harm than help, a fact that would not have been evident in early coding.

You discover you will be working with new equipment. Those who manufacture the equipment with which you would have built your bridge have upgraded their equipment, and your plans won't work using the tools they have sent you. Comparably, software systems are dependent on the technological environment in which they work. Changes in hardware or other companies' software will impact how your software will run. If changes occur, you have to adapt your programs accordingly to work with the new technology.

You are pressed to move faster. The person for whom you are building that bridge wants it done sooner than originally agreed upon. In the software industry, pressure may come from senior management or the marketing department, who want you to work faster to release the product sooner than a competitor releases its product. Pressure to accelerate the schedule could even come from a big customer who has an immediate need for the promised product.

You are working for an overly optimistic developer. The developer is in charge of that bridge you are building, and despite your protestations that there is no way you can complete the project in time, this individual, working on the assumption that luck will be in your favor, sets an unrealistic date by which traffic will be able to cross your bridge. As you go to work one day, where the bridge lies unfinished, you see a bunch of cars stacked up waiting to cross the chasm. Likewise, software developers or those to whom they report may make promises to customers or hype products to the press and, pressured to give a release date, optimistically set unrealistic dates. Cheerleader types, these developers truly think the dates will be made if their team knows they are supportive of their effort—and they'll even put some extra money in their paychecks if they succeed.

You know you can't make the due date, but your supervisor thinks you can if you have more people, and adds people to your team. Each member of the team that has been working on the bridge to date knows his role. But the new people added to the project are underfoot, unsure about what they should be doing. You spend more time handling communications and supervising, and discounting quick fixes the new members of the group recommend. Besides, while there are some things that can be done faster with more people, there are others that can't (think of birthing a baby or writing a book). The same consequences would be experienced if you added more people—no matter how talented—to a software development team. Actually, the more talented they are, the more they might make the first string edgy. And stress has been found to cause almost half of all software errors.

You are asked to have a second level on the bridge you are building, yet complete the project as scheduled. This is another form of scope change that can interfere with completion of a project on schedule. In the case of a bridge, you would have to go back to your blueprints. Likewise, in many software programs, changes in a program under development are requested for whatever reason. There is a story that IBM Corp. saw and liked an operating system being developed for large computer networks. IBM asked for one change—make the system compatible with the gateways of IBM computers. Small change? Not so. The whole system had to be redesigned and 50 percent of the code had to be rewritten. It added a year to the release date.

Oracle's Strategies

The previous examples should give you some insight into the kinds of problems that can occur in product development of software programs. Here are the strategies that Oracle uses to overcome them.

CREATE A SEAMLESS PRODUCT STRATEGY

Despite the hyperbole for which Ellison is known, he and his organization have a sense of the marketplace, and that knowledge serves as a roadmap to direct the company's product development activities. It has been said that Ellison is ahead of market needs by eighteen months. That is, in his mind, as a program is being released, he is already thinking as if it is no longer viable. As one product is being released, his mind is already on another product that is in development. And way before a product is in development, he is thinking about its positioning in the marketplace.

Of course, the plans that Ellison and his management team set are not forged in steel—they couldn't be, given the volatility of the software marketplace—but they do help in

> **Way before a product is in development, Ellison is thinking about its positioning in the marketplace.**

making resource allocation or other tough trade-off decisions, and the like. It has been said that Ellison has the knack of prioritizing, a skill that comes from his prethinking. He and his senior management team—particularly those responsible for product development—regularly meet in a retreat to update their plans.

"Say, wait a minute," you tell me. "I thought that Ellison had a reputation for making promises to audiences about delivery of products not yet under consideration even by Oracle." Yes, there are such occasions. That's when senior management and the development teams come together to develop an action plan to meet the release date promised by Ellison. When Ellison has an idea, like the aggressive competitor that he is, he has a need to thump his chest and tell all how he and his firm, of which he is very proud, will create "this" or "that."

ANTICIPATE THE NEXT WAVE

This is part of the "lock in the customer, lock out the competitor" mantra. It is as fundamental to product development of software programs at Oracle to anticipate customer needs as it is to its sales/customer support initiatives. When you build a product strategy that involves release of new programs, you need to develop not only the platform products but also derivative products. If they aren't finished by release of the first program, they should be in development at the time of release to be ready before competitors enter the market with their products.

As Ellison recognized that he had sold a database to almost every one of the biggest companies in the world, he knew he would need more products to sell. That is how he came up with the idea of applications. Oracle applications would sit on top of and use Oracle databases to perform functions such as inventory management, personnel record keeping, and sales tracking. The proof of his thinking took almost seven years, but by 1995, the company generated nearly $300 million in license revenues from application products and an additional $400 million in applications-related services.

GET GOOD MARKET INFORMATION

Oracle is able to anticipate future needs based on feedback from focus groups, periodic meetings at Oracle's visitor center where customers can talk not only to Oracle's senior management but development managers, and Oracle's annual meeting where customers can describe new needs. The move to the Web and introduction of services such as Oracle MetaLink also allow the company to receive ongoing feedback on existing product shortcomings and new program opportunities (e.g., Club Oracle, users groups, and Oracle chat rooms) from its targeted new market—dot-coms and the bricks and clicks.

HAVE A SENSE OF YOUR CUSTOMERS' NEEDS

When Oracle creates programs, it is clear who the customers are, what they will pay for the program, how long they may use the program, what they plan to use it for, and, most important, how many other current or future customers would be interested in the product. Whenever possible, the company works toward development of programs that have strategic value to its customers. Oracle's first product was introduced in the 1980s, when there were very few standards for computers; each vendor's hardware was different from the next and software was built to work on only one kind of computer or another. Oracle's developers built a product that would work on any computer, thereby minimizing risk both to themselves and to potential customers. They didn't have to bet on which

hardware manufacturer would beat out all the others for dominant position in the marketplace, and large corporate customers with significant computing needs could choose Oracle's
product knowing that they wouldn't have to pay huge amounts

> **Oracle works toward development of pro-
> grams that have strategic value to the
> customers.**

of money to purchase new computers to run the program. The
software application could be adapted (i.e., ported) to run on
a range of computers from different vendors.

CREATE A NEW BUSINESS UNIT FOR NEW MARKETS

Today, there is a program development group within Oracle
that continues to work on the company's flagship (database)
products, and there is a group that specializes on development
of programs that are part of the new e-business market. The
management logic here should be self-evident. Creating a
new business unit allows the core units to stay focused on
their endeavors while at the same time making sure there is
dedicated staff for the new endeavor.

BUILD PROGRAMS WITH FAILURE IN MIND

"Huh?" you say. Yes, Oracle products are designed knowing
that they might fail and that some failure conditions simply
are out of Oracle's control. Given that, Oracle works to

design programs so that damage will be minimal should failure occur. In creating version 5 of its database, for instance, developers created a series of steps to be taken for changes to be made to the data. If the steps are not followed, the database would return to its original state.

HIRE WELL

Oracle looks for the very best people it can find to work on its products, particularly its kernel groups—that is, those groups that are responsible for designing and building Oracle's core database software products. The development that all of the other technical staff at Oracle does is based on the work performed by these groups: moving the database or applications software to new hardware platforms, building development tools, even creating finished software applications. Given the impact that these groups have on Oracle's future, the company makes an extra effort to keep team leaders and members happy—which includes having them participate in strategy discussions about the future of the technology. To develop their knowledge, they are also encouraged to attend research presentations in the industry and given time to install and use competitive products to identify shortcomings.

KEEP SUCCESSFUL TEAMS INTACT

While the rest of the organization undergoes the annual reorganization (as discussed in Chapter 3), not so the kernel teams. The process of building a software product teaches a programmer the pitfalls, so when it is built a second time, it can be built better. One of Oracle's success strategies is to keep the team intact.

KEEP THE KERNEL TEAM FOCUSED ON CORE TECHNOLOGY

The kernel team is encouraged, in particular, to improve the core code, rather than do some extension to the product that may or may not be part of an upcoming release. In an environment where the majority of the company is reorganized on an annual basis, many of the staff involved in designing and building a core product have worked on the last five or six major versions. With that kind of consistency, the team brings all of its experience to the next version of the software.

REWARD THE KERNEL TEAM

The kernel team is rewarded with new and larger grants of stock options. Team members also get lots of attention from senior management—in particular, CEO Larry Ellison. The attention he lavishes on them has a great impact on keeping people on the core team and within Oracle. Roger Bamford is very much a case in point. The rewards he has earned for his programming excellence has made him a multi-millionaire. Regularly courted by Microsoft, he continues to work for Oracle not only for the dollars, but for the respect with which he is held. The company as a whole highly regards these groups for the impact they have on the future of the organization.

IMPLEMENT QUALITY ASSURANCE PRACTICES

Ellison said in 1990 that ". . . quality is a means of competitive advantage."[3] New programs are beta tested with real customers to identify as many bugs as is possible before final release into the marketplace. (Let me add, here, that such beta tests do not eliminate all bugs; new bugs generally surface with each implementation, according to my conversations with IT experts; but Oracle's quality assurance initiative significantly reduces any design defects before release.)

RELEASE EARLY, RELEASE OFTEN

Once a program has been beta tested, it is immediately released into the marketplace. Not only does this ensure that Oracle gets its product in front of customers before competitors, but Oracle's continuous product release process enables it to fine-tune features, one version after another. With each new version, Oracle raises the criteria on which software is judged.

BUILD A CULTURE TO SUPPORT PRODUCT DEVELOPMENT

Have you ever worked for a company that hoards information from its employees? That is, you only know about a new product release when you see an ad in a local newspaper or magazine or it's mentioned on the news. If you worked for Oracle, that would never happen. Oracle does not encourage secrecy when it comes to product releases or schedules. Rather, it floods the organization with the information—and with a purpose. The information is posted with release dates. This sustains the sense of urgency in completing the work on schedule. It also adds to the pride of those development teams whose products are released as planned, and information about their effort is stamped *DELIVERED—ON TIME*.

Management Analysis

I never truly understood the work of software programmers until I talked to those who do it for a living. I have to wonder whether other reporters were as familiar with the work involved as they charged Ellison with half-truths and unkept promises about delivery dates or wrote about bugs in Oracle systems. As I've learned, there are no exceptions to the rule— few products are completed on time and none are created without bugs.

On the other hand, competition is so stiff in the industry that you want to be the first to promise prospective customers a program—consequently, the complaint that Ellison is guilty of hyperbole or talking about programming yet on the drawing board. It's all part of the industry.

CHAPTER SEVEN

CRISES AND MISSTEPS

the perils of fast growth

All fledgling companies experience a moment in their growth when they need to stop and take stock of their operation. When the growth is rapid, it may exert a significant pressure on the organization that it isn't prepared to withstand. The informal systems that drove the growth may be inadequate. It is time to adapt them to reflect the challenge of further growth in the future.

For many companies this moment comes as a surprise. So it was with Oracle. It experienced the hard lessons of growth in the late 1980s. It was a tough time for Oracle, but the lessons learned positioned the firm for even greater growth. The company learned that systems and procedures associated with a mature company would not derail its growth and could coexist with the entrepreneurial culture that had contributed to initial success.

Eric Flamholtz, president of Management Systems Consulting Corp., proposes in his book *Growing Pains: Transitioning from an Entrepreneurship to a Professionally Managed Firm* that organizations go through seven stages in their lives:

New venture

Expansion

Professionalization

Consolidation

Diversification

Integration

Decline and revitalization

With Oracle's decision to develop applications for the Web, it could be said that Oracle has moved into the diversification stage, expanding beyond development of database software. This chapter, however, focuses on expansion, professionalization, and consolidation stages that are central to transforming into a mature business.

The nature of expansion should be self-evident. A company in expansion may be experiencing phenomenal growth (e.g., 100 percent growth in sales annually). Likewise, its sales force may be increasing. Ellison and his management team had identified a market and were creating programs to satisfy customer demands; although there were competitors entering the market daily, and despite the fact that Oracle was a new company, it was the market leader. Unlike the venture stage in which survival is the issue at stake, during expansion the problems are almost directly related to the growth itself. They may influence product quality, customer service, or financial and sales tracking.

As the symptoms of these problems and the consequences of their continuation become evident to management, organizations enter into what Flamholtz calls the professionalization stage. At this stage the organization is formalizing critical processes and installing systems or procedures or practices to undo these problems and prevent their recurrence. Ideally, an

> While a company doesn't set itself up to become a stodgy business, it can grow into one as it expands unless it makes a conscious effort to remain entrepreneurial.

organization should come out of this phase an "entrepreneurially oriented, professionally managed firm," to use Flamholtz's phrase.[1] This transition is never easy. Some organizations suffer severe growing pains, as did Oracle. Its transition changed both the company and Larry Ellison's view of himself as its CEO.

Consolidation is culture-focused. It is when an organization may go in one of two directions. It can retain its entrepreneurial character or it can become bureaucratic and stodgy. While a company doesn't set itself up to become a stodgy business, it can grow into one as it expands unless it makes a conscious effort to remain entrepreneurial through the values and beliefs it promulgates.

It doesn't hurt, either, if the CEO and founder is by nature an entrepreneur, which is certainly the case with Ellison.

Dell's Growing Pains

Before I share with you the Oracle story, let me tell you the story of another entrepreneurial organization as it went through its growing pains. My intent is to demonstrate how common this is for even the most successful of fledgling firms. The company I am spotlighting is Dell Computer Corp., a company whose management success is well known. The tale is told by Michael Dell himself in his book *Direct from Dell.*

Dell's growth problems began in 1989 when, to meet ever-increasing demand for its PCs, it purchased too much inventory. Worse, it had paid a ton of money for 256-kilobyte memory chips that almost overnight had become technologically obsolete as market demand shifted to 1 megabyte. Ridding itself of that inventory depressed its earnings for the quarter to only one cent per share. To compensate, the company raised the price of its PCs, which slowed sales.

Almost immediately thereafter, Dell found itself in another sticky wicket. Perhaps it was too much youthful enthusiasm, but the company expended money and time on a cutting-edge laptop nicknamed Olympic. As aspects of this powerhouse product were released by Dell, it got lukewarm reception from potential customers. Although they found some of the features compelling, the product itself wasn't interesting enough to buy.

The lessons these two experiences taught Dell should be pretty self-evident—and they haven't been forgotten. The value of careful inventory management was taught in the first

> **Dell learned three lessons the hard way.**

situation. The importance of early customer input was learned in the second. The second incident also taught Dell how gradual product improvements were less risky yet would enable it to take advantage of rapid technological transitions.

Two years passed. As the company expanded, it was faced with another conundrum. Should it stay at its current size— $1 billion in sales—or go for the gold ring. Dell chose the gold ring, expanding its sales effort beyond telemarketing to retail chains. Basically, Dell management opted to enter the retail channel because it had become convinced by all those who said the company couldn't continue to grow solely based on direct sales. Other computer manufacturers were selling through retail chains, so why not Dell? Because it was able to handle the Microsoft Windows operating systems just being released, Dell doubled sales before the year was up. Yet, as Michael Dell admitted in his book, while the company was bringing in around $2 billion in sales, it had the infrastructure of a $500 million company. It had outgrown everything from its phone system to its parts numbering system. Staffing was an issue as well. Those on board didn't have the experience to run a $2 billion-plus operation.

The consequences became evident about a year later as management discovered that cash was going out faster than it was coming in. The cause: The company had been operating on the assumption that its sales could grow faster than the market. Rather, it had to focus on slow, steady growth and liquidity. Once it could resolve its liquidity problem, it could refocus on growth, but until then, its focus would have to be, in this order, liquidity, profitability, and finally growth. That meant cancellation of some products in development and, instead, implementation of long-overdue profit-and-loss measurement systems, segmentation of business areas, recruitment of experienced executives who could manage the demands of a maturing business, and the like. As the company checked and rechecked revenue over the next twelve months, segmentation of data revealed how wrong management had been to put resources into the retail business.

Although PC sales were booming, Dell was losing money on each computer it sold that way when you considered the money that went to the distributors. Although the press suggested its decision to exit retail channels would slow Dell's growth, management at Dell knew the direct model (i.e., selling directly to consumers) would save the company money that otherwise would have had to be spent to sell through stores. For example, the continuation of retail distribution would have meant construction of a factory designed specifically to accommodate retail sales. The result was the refocused attention of the entire organization to the business model that had been the foundation of its success as a fledgling business—the direct sales model.

As Dell Computer went through these growing pains, it learned several hard lessons that were the foundation for values and beliefs that remain central to the PC vendor's operations. We're familiar with all of them: Disdain inventory. Always listen to the customer. Never sell indirect. Many of the systems that Dell installed for purposes of better management at that time remain, although they have evolved as the company has evolved. The move to a more professionally run organization never meant that Dell lost its entrepreneurial edge.

The Case of "Growth at All Costs"

Like Dell Computer, Oracle was experiencing ever-increasing growth. Ellison was promoting a "growth at all costs" mind-set, from product development to sales to accounting. As the market leader in relational databases, Oracle's future looked great. Then, in 1990, within a brief period, earnings dropped, programs weren't completed on promised due dates, and version 6 of its relational database was claimed to be "buggy" by customers. Then, as Wall Street learned about some legal but overly aggressive sales and accounting strategies practiced by Oracle that made the company look more successful than it actually was, stock value dropped from almost 30 to a low of 5⅜.

Ellison personally lost over $300 million. He wasn't alone. Many of the early employees who had stock in the company saw their retirement funds disappear. Most important, Oracle seemed on the brink of insolvency. Ellison, who spoke proudly of the talented people his company had, was put into a position of having to order a 10 percent cut in employees across the board, including two senior executives—one in charge of sales, the other the chief financial officer.

The problems could be traced back to the pressure on sales folk to sustain sales growth at 100 percent annually. Take the problem with version 6 of Oracle's database management system (DBMS) released in the late 1980s. As the

> **In 1990, Oracle seemed on the brink of insolvency.**

market leader, Oracle was under constant attack by competitors, and one, Sybase, Inc., had a DBMS with features that Oracle lacked. Although Sybase wasn't a real threat to Oracle, it was getting considerable trade press attention, putting undue pressure on Oracle's sales force that clamored for release of version 6, because this new release had the features that would allow Oracle's DBMS to compete with or surpass Sybase's product. Those in development knew that the program wasn't ready for release, but it was released nevertheless due to the pressure from sales. As word about problems with the program spread, Oracle found itself bashed in the press time and time again.

It wasn't the bugs in the software program alone that eroded Oracle's reputation at the time. To keep up with the increase in sales, Oracle had to grow its support staff accordingly, but many of these technical and customer support employees were new on the job and unfamiliar with Oracle's products. Customers complained that they were transferred from one individual to another, to still another, or waited on the phone for hours until they could talk to someone more familiar with the product than they were. It didn't help, either, when customers, after being bounced from one support person to another, were told that Oracle knew about the problem, had identified the solution, but had not yet gotten around to telling its customers.

Having a first line of support staff that was apparently undertrained and thus largely ineffective was bad enough, but the real problems had to do with a decision to move those individuals responsible for approving sales contracts into the sales department. The argument was made by sales that Oracle's lawyers took too long to review and approve customer contracts, so bringing this part of the work into sales would expedite the process. Ellison accepted the argument, rejecting the concern of financial folk that it was equivalent to putting a fox in charge of the chicken coop.

The financial people proved to be correct. To make their sales quotas, sales personnel would commit to weak deals—offering extended payment terms and selling to cash-poor customers, for example. Consequently, money came in slowly, if at all, for sales made. Whereas the industry average for collection was about sixty days, Oracle was taking an average of 200 days to collect from customers in the United States. Oracle's record-keeping system also enabled it to erroneously credit as actual sales software products in distributor warehouses awaiting purchase; product paid for yet not delivered (sometimes still in development); shipment of incomplete product; and income in one year for income due over several years based on promise of a deep discount. At the same time, Oracle was spending money as if it were printing its own to hire people and open new offices. The year before Oracle had sales of $583 million and $262 in receivables. In 1990, it had $970 million in revenue and $468 in uncollected bills. From a record-keeping perspective, Oracle booked revenue a quarter ahead of itself, on the assumption that only a few, if any, of its current customers would return their Oracle products and ask for a refund. A problem wouldn't occur as long as 1) revenue would continue to grow year after year, 2) customers paid up as expected, and 3) none of the customers returned product. These three things didn't happen.

The situation came to a head in spring 1990 during a senior management meeting. Ellison was told that $15 million worth of revenue was essentially fictional. It would seem that one side argued to book the revenue; the bean counters pointed to the shaky deals made and argued it wouldn't be the right thing to do to credit these sales as real income. Until shown the proof, Ellison chose to do the right thing for Oracle and his shareholders and acknowledge the shortfall.

The actual announcement was made on March 27, 1990. In a press release, Oracle announced that third quarter revenues had increased 54 percent, but in a paragraph about midway into the document it also observed that profits had increased only one percent over the quarter of the year before. Ellison was quoted as saying, "We were disappointed with a $15 million shortfall."[2] The next day, the stock for Oracle plummeted.

There was speculation that Ellison would have to quit, as nineteen shareholders filed class-action lawsuits for securities fraud and the Securities and Exchange Commission (SEC)

> "To sue Oracle, please press 3, to sue Larry Ellison personally, press 4."

launched an investigation into the company's accounting and billing practices. Steve Jobs, Ellison's best friend, told the press that his friend's main phone number should answer with the following message: "To sue Oracle, please press 3, to sue Larry Ellison personally, press 4." The situation was muddied when news arose that several Oracle directors and executives had sold stock for which they significantly profited.

Ellison wasn't one of those executives, but he was still accused in the suit of acquiescing in the conduct—as if he had control over their personal actions.

Years later, in recalling what happened, Ellison told his biographer: "I didn't know how serious a problem we had. Had I been a more seasoned executive, I would have known several quarters before that we had problems."[3] Ellison didn't

> **Ellison probably wouldn't have listened had he been forewarned that the company's growth was outpacing its ability to manage it.**

like bean counters—he did like the sales group and its VP— so it is unlikely if he would have listened had he been forewarned that the company's growth was outpacing its ability to manage it. More attention to finances was needed, not less, but Ellison had his eye on the marketplace and competitors coming at Oracle from every direction. The settlement in the end cost Oracle $24.1 million. Beyond that, it taught Ellison a lesson about the danger of rapid growth distracting from the need to attend to internal operations and corporate infrastructure. Ellison learned that an eye on the shop was needed— for everything from product development to customer relationships. He may also have asked himself if that was the role he should play considering his subsequent actions.

Lessons Learned from Oracle and Dell

In many respects, the stories of Dell Computer and Oracle are similar. Although the specific circumstances are different, both entrepreneurs got so caught up in pursuing fast growth that they lost control briefly of their businesses. Flamholtz rightfully named his book on the lifecycle of companies *Growing Pains*, especially if you think of these two corporate case studies in particular. Both companies experienced the painful consequences of business booms. Fortunately, both companies had at their helm strong executives who could acknowledge the situation and install the kinds of internal systems to prevent repetitions of the problems.

Just as Dell went outside to hire experienced executives—those who had worked previously in mature companies—so, too, did Ellison. When Ellison hired Jeff Henley to assert control over the operations side of the business, many considered the new CFO to be Oracle's savior. Yet Henley wouldn't have joined Oracle if Ellison hadn't had the guts to admit that he failed to keep his finger on the pulse of an important part of the business. Ultimately, Ellison demonstrated the business smarts to acknowledge that this aspect of the business was better left in the hands of someone who could give the area the attention it needed. It may have been around this time that Ellison began to rethink his role as CEO, as the external presence of Oracle in the marketplace, the Barnum with rosy possibilities and promises about future products to separate Oracle from its competitors (the visionary or "oracle" at Oracle). In 1992, Ellison brought in another outsider—Ray Lane—to take over sales. Lane worked closely with Ellison to bring Oracle through the professionalization process, as Flamholtz terms it.

Spending restraint and careful tracking of sales weren't the only lessons that came from the experience. Out of it came, too, a recognition of the importance of product quality and customer care. Within Oracle, the added emphasis on quality may have been met with some resentment by individuals who felt they had done just that all along. However, in the outside world it took attention away from the precarious financial situation Oracle had gone through. Moving away from its previous cavalier attitude toward product release, Oracle instituted a product testing process, which in turn led in time to more thorough product testing and recognition of the highest level of product quality and processes in the form of International Standards Organization (ISO) certification.

Consolidation

The 1990s crisis also added specific values to the ones that already existed. Added to the mantras "crush the competition" and "lock customers in, lock competitors out" was a new one: "Spend money on what matters." Another is to "think like a stockholder" and, most important, to "fix the mistake and move on." In Oracle's case, over the next years, revenue doubled each year—$2 billion in 1992, $4 billion in 1994, $6 billion in 1996, and $8 billion in 1998.

Coincidentally or not, it was during these years that Ellison recognized that the flagship business of Oracle had limited growth and new opportunities needed to be found to continue to expand the business. The company had weath-

> **Fix the mistake and move on.**

ered the crisis, and in Ellison's view it was time to move beyond a one-product company. It didn't help that a study Ellison sponsored had found that among *Wall Street Journal* readers, the name Oracle meant little. Less than one percent had any knowledge of the fourth-largest software company at the time. Consequently, Ellison instituted a program to build brand awareness for Oracle. After all, brand awareness is key to sustaining market leadership.

Over the years since, Oracle has invested heavily in building a worldwide brand. Ellison had a specific purpose: to link Oracle's name to cutting-edge products. At the time, Apple was the only company people felt connected with. Ellison wanted that same kind of immediate connection in customers' minds for Oracle. His plan was to tie the company's business value proposition together with its brand name.

For SAP AG, the brand value proposition can be found on its Web site. "We don't just make better software. We make better companies," the company asserts, thereby pointing to the claim that the "open interfaces" in SAP's software enable communication among legacy systems, SAP systems, and external systems, providing "enormous scalability and flexibility." Oracle's efforts play up its software's "manageability," in addition to the firm's leadership position in "thinking up new ideas." Ellison became the voice for Oracle, predicting program after program to come from Oracle to spur IT's interest.

The Dream of the Network Computer

Many initiatives preceded Ellison's concept of a network computer. Oracle talked about interactive TV and about purchasing Apple Computer, Inc. These ideas, among others, may have been attempts to bring the company name to the consciousness of the average consumer more than they were serious initiatives.

There was no question, though, that Ellison saw one concept—the network computer—as a means of growing the company to that stage Flamholtz terms *diversification*. Rather than buy PCs, customers could buy Oracle-developed workstation hardware and software that was designed to run Oracle database applications. Less expensive than a PC, the network computer was a $500 device that would sit on your desk with display and memory but no hard or floppy disk drives. There would be two ports—one for power and the other to connect to the network. The appliances Oracle would produce would be designed to run only one application that could be loaded from across the network, eliminating the cost of diskettes or CD-ROMs and thereby reducing further the cost of a workstation. When the network connection was made, the latest version of the operating system would automatically be downloaded. Files would be stored on a server somewhere in the network and would be backed up every night by people paid to do so. "All of this [storage, access, and backup] would be paid for through my phone bill because that's what the computer really is—an extension of my telephone. I can use it for computing, communication, and entertainment," said Ellison.[4]

If the idea worked, Oracle would own the entire computer infrastructure—from hardware to software—and Microsoft would no longer have a stranglehold on the Internet software market. Oracle would provide the soft-

> "I think personal computers are ridiculous."

ware that linked all the diskless computers into the global network. In Ellison's opinion, Microsoft was so focused on the traditional standalone PC that it had ignored creation of such software.

Oracle programmers had estimated it would take around a year to make the network computer a reality, though a working prototype would be developed in a few months. Yet Ellison in his confrontation at a Paris conference with Gates, promised delivery in a few month's time. He not only hinted about Oracle's plan, he told competitors, customers, and through the press at the conference, the world.

Oracle's CEO told the conference attendees, "I think personal computers are ridiculous...Why should I have to go to a store to buy software! It's a box of bits; not only that, they are old bits. The software you buy at a store is hardly ever the latest release."[5]

The network computer never was a success, but there may be other lessons it taught Ellison, the entrepreneur. For one, don't overdesign a good idea. When the idea was first pre-

> **Before the idea was even on the drawing board, Ellison gave the show away.**

sented to him, Ellison began to rethink it and considered how he could take Microsoft head-on, with a word processing package, spreadsheet, e-mail, and a Web browser. The original idea of a one-application device evolved into a substitute for a Windows PC, an idea that would demand more study and time to prototype and produce.

More important, to quote a World War II slogan, "loose lips sink ships." Before the idea was even on the drawing board, Ellison gave the show away at the Paris conference.

Ellison has been known for being "loose-lipped" throughout his career. According to industry experts, in most instances his company already has a project under development when he announces it. Although it puts unnecessary pressure on developers, it doesn't endanger the project. Customers actually appreciate knowing what's on the drawing board at Oracle because that means by the time they need the product Oracle would have it ready for them. This wasn't the situation with the network computer, though.

The strategy seemed unclear to the press, and that's how they reported it. Customers had serious concerns about the implications to their current setups. If Oracle was to sell these network appliances, who would support them? How would the software applications running on the Oracle computer compare to those running on the Microsoft Windows program? Oracle didn't have answers to those questions—at least, as they were being asked.

More important, Bill Gates had been in the audience as Ellison shared his idea with the world. Gates knew the answers to the hard questions that the press and customers were asking, and his replies made the overly enthusiastic Ellison look as if he were talking out of his hat. Ellison was just precipitous. Microsoft heard a challenge when it was issued, and Gates and his management team rallied their people together to make Oracle's network computer announcement appear impossible.

Management Analysis

Truth is, Gates saw that the idea Oracle was proposing could work. If Oracle didn't deliver, Apple or Hewlett-Packard Co. might be able to overcome the deficiencies that Oracle had identified. So Microsoft went on the offensive, reducing the cost of PCs, improving PC usability, and improving PC administration. As Microsoft addressed the weaknesses that Ellison had spotlighted, at Oracle the project continued to grow. All of a sudden the vision for the network computer included set-top boxes that brought the Internet to a TV and screen phones optimized for consumer access to the Internet. Rather than putting a division in charge of product development, as was done in the past with successful products, Oracle formed an independent company—Network Computer, Inc. (NCI)—to focus on the network computer. Staff joining the company received stock in Oracle, not NCI, which likely created mixed loyalty, as many had one foot in Oracle and one in NCI.

The product wasn't even built before Oracle was selling it. That only added to the problem because Oracle's sales force knew how to sell expensive software, not the inexpensive pieces of hardware with software included.

Needless to say, the network computer never had a chance. Why have I included it in a chapter on making the transformation to a mature business? Because Ellison, with his network computer concept, had taken on a mature market with the intention of unseating the leader. Ellison should have come away with two lessons. First and foremost, Oracle must continue to look for new businesses (see Chapters 9 and 10) in which it may have to confront the biggest players in that market. However, when you take on a mature market, you have to play by the rules of the marketplace. Second, you can be an entrepreneur and sustain an entrepreneurial culture within your organization, but you have to pursue new market opportunities less as a visionary and more as a ruthless competitor.

P A R T

3

WHERE DO THE
ORACLES GO
FROM HERE?

CHAPTER EIGHT

WALKING THE TALK

oracle moves to the web

Although Oracle's network computer never

took off, Larry Ellison retained his vision of a future without Microsoft Corp., but one dependent on Oracle database technology. And with cause. In the late 1990s, his firm was experiencing pressure on two fronts. First and foremost, its flagship marketplace was becoming smaller. Research by Dataquest of the database market in 1996 showed that sales that year grew 20 percent; by 1997 they would slow to half that rate; by 2000, Dataquest forecasted that the figure might be halved once again. Second, and no doubt personally frustrating to Ellison, Microsoft (under the direction of his "nemesis" Bill Gates) had aggressively entered the market with a rival product to Oracle's database. Microsoft SQL Server sold at a much lower cost compared to Oracle's product. Microsoft was positioned to attack Oracle's database market share.

After much work on Ellison's part in convincing an otherwise uncertain management team about the advisability of doing so, Ellison and his top executives agreed on a new future for Oracle, one in which it would become a supplier of Internet-based applications. Furthermore, it would become a brick-and-click business itself.

In spring 2000, Oracle unveiled its E-Business Suite, combining a number of Internet applications in a single package in the same manner that Microsoft sold once-separate PC applications (e.g., word processor, spreadsheet, database, etc.) to consumers in a single box. Oracle's E-Business Suite included seventy "modules" for Internet use, including enterprise resource planning (which covers human resources management and accounting) and customer relationship management (which handles front-office operations such as sales force automation and customer data management). Since then, the number of software applications has grown, but the original marketing approach has remained. Customers may buy the entire suite or purchase parts of it online or on disks. Ideally, Oracle will "host" the applications, letting customers tap into information via the Web. Customer firms that prefer to use their own servers get updates electronically. Furthermore, customers don't have to buy a new package every eighteen months; they can pay a subscription fee to receive updates every quarter.

With this move, Oracle is still very much in the business of selling software, but its approach is very different from the past because the focus is away from the product *per se* and is more toward offering management solutions to customers. The goal of the company is to integrate multiple Oracle products into a complete solution that will enable a customer to manage information worldwide through the Internet.

The business change also has meant a change in Ellison's work style. In 1999, Ellison, known to take time off work to pursue the life of a playboy, became hands-on, spearheading

> **The goal of the company is to integrate multiple Oracle products into a complete solution.**

program development and the subsequent transformation of his business. As CEO, Ellison believed the change process needed his leadership. Ray Lane, promoted to president of the company in 1996, found himself with less and less to do. At least that is one explanation for his decision to resign. Another story is that Lane led the faction initially opposed to Ellison's vision of Oracle developing applications for the Web. Still another is that Ellison believed that Lane lacked the dynamic personality to drive the move to the Web.

The business rumor is that Ellison wanted to stop development on all of Oracle's traditional programs to focus the full attention of the business, from Oracle's staff of program developers to its sales force, on Web applications. In the end, at least half of Oracle's developers and all its sales force were assigned to work on the Internet applications. The company acknowledged that at first its executives fought the move, worried about possible glitches. "But Larry had the power of his conviction," Jeremy Burton, an Oracle senior vice president, told the press.[1] Ellison admitted, "This is a new idea. It will take a while for it to be understood by the marketplace—or even by our own sales force. . . . It takes a while for any new idea—whether it's Galileo's or ours—to get accepted. We are faced with the same problem that Galileo had," he declared.[2] In an interview with *Fortune* magazine's Brent Schlender, Ellison went further, admitting that he had put "Internetization" into motion in 1997 before going on his summer vacation. Upon his return, he had discovered that the jobs weren't getting done. Software developers were only paying lip service to creation of the product line. Longstanding customers were being assured that Oracle wouldn't pull the plug on client/server applications. It was these circumstances that prompted his decision to take a more active role in the transition. "Apparently I hadn't convinced everyone how serious I was."[3]

Despite Ellison's many claims in the past that had proven untrue (from unseating Microsoft with network computers to purchasing Apple Computer, Inc.) and his reputation as a chronic exaggerator (consider even his comparison of his decision to build Web-based applications to Galileo's announcement that the world revolved around the sun), the market seemed to buy the idea. After all, if Oracle could do what it promised, chief information officers (CIOs) reasoned that their companies' management would be able to track, analyze, and control the behavior of each business unit, even each employee, not only nationally but globally, in real time via the Internet. The global network that Oracle was promis-

> **Oracle's strategy: Win the war on complexity.**

ing it could deliver would give senior management greater control at less cost than current PC-supported Internet systems demanded. Asked about Ellison's plan, long-time friend Steve Jobs, founder of Apple Computer, told reporters that Microsoft had been caught off guard, distracted by its competition with Netscape Communications Corp. (which in time became part of America Online). Oracle had had the time to position itself to compete face-to-face with Microsoft. Rightly or wrongly, Ellison came out punching with his idea of network computing, but that hadn't worked. Instead, it morphed into what Jobs referred to as "server computing," which he thought Oracle was well positioned to offer.

No question, Oracle's "strategy for winning the war on *complexity*" (the term complexity referring to Microsoft's approach to the Internet) was easily bought into by corporate leaders based on the day-to-day problems they were encountering. In essence, Oracle and Ellison were telling businesses that to be competitive in a 24/7 world market, they needed to centralize all their information into a single global data source, accessible from anywhere in the world with a standard Web browser. The Oracle strategy was based on successful growth of the ever-growing dot-coms. Despite their downfall, the idea still had merit. The Internet still had business value, and Ellison could promise to help legacy and click-and-mortar businesses use the Web to improve access and communicate information across their own operations as well as with their customers and vendors.

A New Commitment

There's a personal reason why Ellison would support this idea. If you visit Oracle's Web site, you can read a document entitled "Primer: Win the War on Complexity" that points to the value of having access to information from within and outside, from vendors and customers, nationally and globally (the Dell model) rather than from disparate information systems. The message is meant for prospective and current customers, but it is one that could just as well have applied to Ellison and his team prior to the crisis of 1990. If Oracle had had access to the kind of information that its new E-Business Suite promises, the 1990 crisis might never have occurred, a fact that I am sure has not been lost on Ellison. With or without the aid of bean counters, he and his senior executives would have known about the cavalier deals being struck by the sales force that in turn led to cash flow problems, late delivery, and poor program quality.

Of the time spent in developing the first applications for the E-Business Suite, Ellison told the press, "I love running the business now . . . I love getting involved in every detail of the business. I was never interested in the sales force before. Now we control the sales force or choreograph the sales force by using computers. It's all programmed."[4] His enthusiasm is understandable. Ellison may not dress or act like a "geek," but he shares their enthusiasm for new technology. His management side, too, appreciates the business benefits that use of the technology should reap—and the impact it would have on Oracle's long-term growth. The showman side of his personality, the Barnum side, recognizes the marketing potential of the technology.

As I am writing this book, the economy has declined as the implications of a war, even a sporadic one against terrorist factions, hovers. Competition for the new business that Ellison had identified continues to exist, with Microsoft and IBM Corp., both giants in their own areas. They are still competing for the position of dominant player in the high end and middle of the applications market, which is also where Oracle has positioned itself. The future is unclear. Pre-September 11, 2001, the selling mantra, "Get a suite" rang through the halls of Oracle while other best-of-breed software developers—that is, developers of software that address the management information needs of companies addressed via the Oracle applications in its E-Business Suite—were seeking deals with IBM and Microsoft to help market their products to corporate customers. For example, Siebel Systems, Inc., under former Oracle executive Tom Siebel, had partnered with IBM, which is selling a package competitive with the Oracle E-Business Suite but made up of best-of-breed software programs from various vendors. The best-of-breed approach recommends third-party offerings available in the marketplace instead of steering customers to a proprietary package. Post-September 11 results will depend on the impact that the threat of a war will have on the general health of the business community in general, which will influence technology purchases, as well as competitive strategies of each market player.

Oracle's e-business software suite began with three product groups for customer relationship management (CRM), e-business, and business-to-business (B2B) functions. CRM is for the sale side, the e-business product is used for internal applications, and B2B for the buy side. Under these product groups are more than seventy applications and software modules. Oracle suspects smaller firms will choose the suites sooner than large firms because it is too costly and time-consuming for larger firms to do a system overhaul. Ultimately, however, even the largest companies may recognize that they can manage more efficiently and effectively, and thereby save money over the longer term, by ripping out everything and doing it right the first time rather than remaining dependent on "software kits," the term Oracle uses to refer to best-of-breed packages. It's not clear just how companies will, as a practical matter, want to do that when systems in the Oracle E-Business Suite must align with current processes—so customers must reengineer their processes on a massive scale to

> **Ultimately even the largest companies may recognize that they can save money over the longer term by ripping out everything and doing it right the first time.**

use the E-Business Suite. Indeed, that may explain why few customers were purchasing the entire suite when it was first released, choosing instead individual programs within the suite as need existed.

According to Bob Lewis of *InfoWorld*, "The good news is that the process designs themselves are done. The bad news is that the good news only covers about 10 percent of the total effort of changing every process of your company."[5]

What makes this move by Oracle intriguing is not the new products but how creation of those products has changed Oracle itself. Lane, describing Oracle's own transformation to an e-business, sums up my key point: "What Larry is doing is much more than putting on the world's largest e-commerce demo. He's looking at how the fundamental structure of our company should change to take advantage of what Internet computing will enable—just as other CEOs should be doing."[6] Ellison chose to practice what he preached, incorporating the applications of the Oracle E-Business Suite into his own operations and transforming Oracle into a brick-and-click operation comparable to Dell Computer Corp. For this reason, the experience is worthy of study by executives, regardless of what happens to application sales.

In any event, as of Fall 2001, the applications business represents only about one-tenth of Oracle's revenues; however, Ellison has placed the future of his business on the line, reinventing it as a B2B player in the software business. For an organization that was expected to be buried by the Internet as companies found cheaper and simpler ways of managing their data on the Web, Oracle is becoming quite a success story. Success comes not only from selling enterprise e-business software, but in using that same software to enhance its own business.

Key to that success isn't just Oracle's products but the well-being of the Internet—and the likelihood of another dot-com revolution. As mentioned, Ellison's strategy was built not only on the move by larger organizations to the Web but on the growth of the myriad dot-coms that populated it in the mid- to late 1990s. The dot-com shakeout destroyed that opportunity. Prior to the terrorist attacks on the United States on September 11, 2001, industry analysts predicted a recurrence—a whole new infusion of dot-coms with better, well-considered business plans. But those projections were based on the assumption that the economy would quickly revive and revenue would be available.

The market situation is more muddied as I write this.

Eat Your Own Product

Whatever happens in the marketplace, Oracle is now its own customer.

After studying the impact that centralizing information and automating relationships with customers would have on a business, Ellison announced to Oracle's board and the world at large that by implementing the applications he would be marketing, Oracle could cut costs by a half billion dollars in a year. Early results prompted him to up that number to $1 billion, or about 10 percent of Oracle's revenue, a commitment that generated a lot of press for the firm—and its new product line. It was an opportunity that the P. T. Barnum quality in Lawrence J. Ellison couldn't ignore.

Just as Barnum brought Tom Thumb and Jumbo to Washington, D.C. and paraded them before thousands and thousands of spectators in the mid 1800s, in 2000 Larry Ellison could stand before members of the business press and show them an operating statement that indicated a $1 billion savings. For the fiscal year ending May 31, 2000, profits had jumped 61 percent, to $1.2 billion. Operating expenses had dropped nearly $1 billion below where they would have been had they grown at the same rate as sales. There are doubters—in the press, in the investment community, and among corporate analysts. Charles Phillips of Morgan Stanley Dean Witter, for one, says at least one-third of the margin improvement may have come from a shift in the sales mix to higher-margin software products from less profitable consulting services, as well as from the layoff of numbers of consultants as major software installations for customers were completed. Even a savings of two-thirds of $1 billion is worth crowing about, though.

However, the story isn't the cost savings, but how the savings came to be.

Even for Ellison, a man known for his focused approach to management, it wasn't easy to rebuild his company to achieve those savings, and rebuild it is exactly what was involved, just as Michael Dell rebuilt Dell Computer when he put its entire operation on the Web.

Once again, a comparison of the two men and their organizations are in order. Michael Dell, like Ellison, met with internal obstacles—from members of his management team and his telesales force. Moving his business to the Internet represented a massive change, too, but it enabled Dell to build partnerships with customers and vendors. The company's goal—to improve the total customer experience—was achieved based on customer feedback. There were also obvious financial savings as the company shifted away from telemarketing to servicing customers via the Web, both in terms of new orders and customer support. In his book *Direct from Dell*, Michael Dell suggests that going virtual enabled his company to expand the business further, but unlike an earlier time, it experienced *controlled* hypergrowth using the management information accessible via the Internet.

Dell's move to the Web can be seen as a move in the corporate lifecycle model described by Eric Flamholtz in his book *Growing Pains* (see Chapter 7). In Flamholtz's opinion, companies move through various stages, from new ventures all the way to companies in decline undergoing revitalization. Infrequently have I seen such clear-cut shifts, first by Dell, and more recently by Oracle. The model reflects a process that companies must undertake to support further growth once they have become mature organizations.

Dell's move to the Web represented the sixth stage—integration. In moving to the Web, Dell changed the sales channel, but he also rebuilt his business to operate on the Web. Ellison's company would seem to have undergone two stages

> **Oracle's transformation required changes in operational systems, management systems, even corporate culture.**

in the Flamholtz model—stage five, diversification in its development of a new line of products (i.e., a move away from being a one-product company), and stage six, integration of the business as a whole via the Web. Oracle began by expanding its product line to sell Internet-based software, but the ultimate result was transformation of Oracle into a business that could support the products it sold; that meant changes in its internal operational systems, management systems, and even corporate culture.

In his book *E-Business or Out of Business: Oracle's Roadmap for Profiting in the New Economy*, Mark J. Barrenechea, senior vice president for applications development at Oracle, observes that the challenge of the Internet is for companies to re-create themselves on the Internet through the use of applications and application suites. The end-product is a site where a company can sell, deliver, and service customers globally, efficiently and effectively, and access its own databases that enable better internal management.

Oracle Goes Web

Ellison recognized that Oracle technology needed to be redesigned so it could be deployed over the Internet. Around the same time, he saw the opportunity that the Internet offered if he could reengineer Oracle Corp.'s business operations for the Web. That meant using, within Oracle, the same technology his firm sold. If his plan worked he would be doing away with specific and complex applications software and, instead, managing business processes via simple standardized Internet browsers. Both information technology (IT) staff and costs could be cut if data could be crunched on a few giant servers then controlled and displayed through a browser. From a management perspective, it would be easier for company executives to get information about their business in an instant.

As CEO of the company, Ellison later admitted, he didn't even know how many employees the company actually had worldwide. That fact only became known, according to Barrenechea, because Ellison had asked the question. Ellison was getting a demo from the human resources development team during which they pointed to the fact that it took fewer keystrokes to create a record for a new employee using the Oracle application than it did for PeopleSoft's application. Ellison stopped the demo for a moment to ask the team to show him how many employees Oracle had and how their skills were distributed among product revenue and service support lines. The team couldn't answer the questions. All of Oracle's information was in Oracle databases, but there were too many of them. "We had hundreds of large server computers managing hundreds of separate databases," Ellison recalled in the preface to Barrenechea's book.[7]

For instance, there were six separate customer databases—marketing, Web store, telesales, field sales, accounting, and services. There were 100 customer databases around the world as well. France had six, as did Japan and Brazil. There were multiple customer databases in every country in which Oracle did business, and Oracle does business in more than 150 countries. In addition, there were 140 product and pricing databases, 70 separate human resource databases, and 97 e-mail databases. Every country had its own data center with computer hardware and IT staff maintaining separate systems for marketing, sales, and service. Each country manager had his own e-mail, human resources, and financial reporting systems, supported by 43 data centers. There were 70 accounting systems in 70 different countries. Rather than improve the situation, each time a new computer system and database were added anywhere within Oracle's worldwide operations, the information became more fragmented—and tougher to use to gain insight into the big business picture.

Ellison immediately concluded that Oracle had to build a "global system" and "unfragment our data."[8] He also realized the opportunity this presented; if Oracle had this problem, so did most global businesses.

To resolve the problem, Ellison deduced that he had to move Oracle's business processes onto the Internet and its information onto a global database. To take advantage of the business opportunity, he ordered that every enterprise-software product be converted to work on the Internet and manipulated on a PC or other "network appliance" via a browser. He also decreed that work stop on development of all client/server products. The sales force was told to inform customers that Oracle would phase out those products by 2000.

Silos

The situation that Ellison encountered seems simple enough, but to create Oracle.com, Ellison had to break down silos, functional and global, but in particular global silos. He decided that the firm would have two data centers, one in headquarters and a backup in Colorado Springs, and one global database for each major function. He recalled, "Passive resistance broke out everywhere."[9]

To reduce the resistance, Ellison began with the simplest of systems, Oracle's e-mail setup, which was well received because it saved money and worked faster. It led to release of other global Internet-based applications that gave customers and/or employees access to information from a single database through an Internet browser. In time, the company developed eleven programs, each handling a single function—from order management to purchasing—that the company began to sell in May 2000. More important, it began to use these systems itself.

Oracle did more than globalize its systems; it globalized the business itself. For instance, multiple IT organizations throughout the world were centralized into a single operation. In essence, Ellison told country managers they could retain control over IT, but they would have to pay for it out of country sales. As IT operations became centralized, this led to huge economies of scale, not only in labor but also in purchasing computer equipment and network services. It cost less than the old network yet the new network was much faster and more reliable.

This move was also essential for Oracle's e-business transformation. Sales and marketing went on the Internet. So did service support. Several global databases let "customers do everything for themselves," according to Mark Jarvis, senior vice president of marketing. "We make our customers enter their own bug reports. That saves us money because we don't have people sitting by telephones."[10] The global sales database not only lowers costs—from $350 per sales call to $20 via the Web site—but it improves the accuracy of orders. Sales expense reports also are submitted online, reducing processing costs from $60 to $10. Online training has reduced the cost of customer training from $250 per head (for off-site training at hotels) to $2 per person.

The process of aligning e-business strategies with corporate strategies involved what Oracle labeled "leader-led change." In essence, Ellison personally dedicated himself to leading all activities dealing with broad-based e-business ini-

> **Oracle did more than globalize its systems; it globalized the business itself.**

tiatives, and he institutionalized e-teams to work on critical parts of the transformation. As part of the process, Oracle had a standing Executive Committee Meeting every Thursday to review how to integrate e-business into each line of business. In addition, the company has set up annual meetings of key players and members of senior management to celebrate the previous year's e-business performance and define the top-three goals for the year and top-ten steps for attaining those goals. There is also an All Managers Call monthly, a conference call on Internet simulcast. This meeting lasts up to two hours. About one-third of the time is spent with the senior vice president of support services sharing key messages about e-business. The remainder of the time is available for Q&A.

Oracle's Global Management Team for Support Services, made up of support personnel and more than 100 managers, meets every six weeks. Ellison provides the vision, and the team is responsible for executing that vision.

One-Stop Shopping

A first visit to the Oracle.com site can be confusing, but my comfort level has grown with each visit. At the Oracle site, I can enroll in a university program or subscribe to an online training service. I can purchase software or request information about a specific application—traditional or e-business. As a customer, I can get support for a software problem or the telephone number of a live person, if I prefer, to help me. For those in IT, there are also stories about corporate applications of Oracle programs, and audio and video clips to keep them alert to trends and the latest product information. An outsider can see the broad range of products and services available through Oracle. An insider—an Oracle manager—can do the job better with the information available directly and indirectly through the applications available as a result of Oracle's move to the Web.

Management Analysis

Ellison's vision for Oracle is dependent on the future of the Internet and a second dot-com revolution—which in turn is dependent on the economy. His company also has stiff competition, from major players and upstarts. On the other hand,

Ellison and Oracle are after a major share of what could be a $70 billion market, which would seem worth the risk.

Initial results are weak because of present corporate spending on technology, but the strategy seems sound. Before the September 11, 2001, tragedy there were projections that another boom would begin by the start of 2002 and, with it, a new dot-com revolution with firms with realistic business plans and staying power. That would be the perfect scenario for Oracle's plan to host e-businesses.

CHAPTER NINE

AN EXTRA-ORDINARY MAN

Ellison as manager, leader, visionary

The press and public have become so obsessed with Larry Ellison's personality that they ignore three conclusions I have reached after considerable research:

Larry Ellison is an excellent manager.

Larry Ellison is an excellent leader.

Larry Ellison is a visionary able to anticipate the demands of his customers in the future and make them a reality.

Let me add a fourth, which is really an addendum to this chapter yet could easily get lost in talk about Ellison's commitment to his company, his mansions, and MiG jets, let alone his management ability: Ellison is also a philanthropist who has endowed an institution to provide vaccines to combat infectious diseases in the Third World. Called the Ellison Medical Foundation, it also funds research into finding cures for diseases of the elderly. He is also owner of 70 percent of a research firm called Quark Biotech, Inc. with more than 100 PhDs. The firm isn't just commercializing new kinds of gene diagnostics—it is also seeking a cure for cancer. I only recently learned about these two Ellison initiatives. Known for his effort in self-promotion and—more so—promotion of Oracle Corp., Ellison hasn't committed any PR to the foundation bearing his name. Nor does he say much about Quark Biotech, Inc., the Israeli start-up in which he has majority ownership.

What Makes a Good Manager, Leader, and Visionary

To be sure that we are on the same page, let me share my definitions of a good manager, good leader, and good visionary.

A hands-on manager will work with employees to get the work done. A participative manager will meet with employees to determine the tactics they will use to achieve the group's goals. But a manager doesn't have to be participative in style to be a good manager. Autocrats make good managers as well. Indeed, the best managers adapt their style to meet the needs of their employees—it's called situational management. However they supervise, good managers know how to delegate work to others, which, most important, means they know those factors that motivate and use that knowledge to get the highest productivity from workers. Good managers are very focused on the work before them.

Leaders, on the other hand, have a broader perspective. Their focus is on the mission to be achieved. Toward it, they have the ability to influence others to follow them. The secret of good leadership is skill in achieving followership, which means that charisma, though not required, doesn't hurt. Good leaders are decisive, addressing problems as they crop up. In addition, they determine the corporate culture and the values or beliefs that are to be practiced within the organization.

A leader sets the vision, which is different from being visionary. A vision is a clear, consistent course reading for the organization—the purpose for the organization. In sharing that vision or shared wish for the future of the organization, the leader hopes to inspire and motivate all to work toward its achievement. In hard times or times of change, as we are experiencing now, that vision can be a potent weapon against fear—to use another seafarer's analogy, like a rudder, it keeps the corporate ship and its crew on course.

What makes a visionary? In the business world, it's someone who predicts a major direction in which an industry is likely to move. In the case of Larry Ellison, while the tactics have changed, the prediction hasn't. If you separate the ramblings, self-absorbed remarks, and highly entertaining ad libs, his vision for the future is pretty much the same: software applications shared over a network, and hardware designed and priced to serve those needs.

Larry Ellison, Excellent Manager

When you write a book about an executive, you begin with the basics, such as the individual's place of birth, schooling, first business experiences, and so forth. (In fact, those details of Ellison's life are covered in Chapter 1.) Although your focus is on the business side, you begin to learn much more about your subject. So it has been with my study of Larry Ellison. Early on, as I first began to prepare for this book, I knew only about Ellison's pursuit of the good life. Yacht racer, jet pilot, epicure—I had heard him called the "playboy of the wired world." Yet, as I have come to realize, there is a serious side to Ellison—he is, after all, running one of the world's largest software companies and, rightfully, chasing Bill Gates.

Think about it. Microsoft Corp. became a public source of contention in the mid-1990s when Oracle offered the network computer to the marketplace; this was Oracle's way to directly compete with Bill Gates's lordship of the Internet. For the same reason, expect to hear in the future that Ellison has taken on the minions of IBM Corp., as well as Gates, since they now represent a threat to his company in the applications software market. Maybe even Hasso Plattner, CEO of German software developer SAP, will come in for some of Ellison's verbal abuse during a press conference. Already a visit to *www.oracle.com* reveals documents that question IBM's capability to provide Web applications and SAP's talent in hosting sites.

Over the years, Ellison may have made the wrong decision or taken the wrong turn, personally or professionally—who hasn't? Yet throughout his life, since he founded the company that today bears the name Oracle, he has been fully committed to its success.

There is an Ellison story that confirms his reputation as a womanizer yet simultaneously demonstrates the importance of Oracle in the scheme of things. It was just after the 1990 crisis, and Ellison received a telephone call from one of his senior managers. Ellison was asked if the manager had Ellison's approval to terminate his secretary. She had a record of poor performance, and unless Ellison disagreed, her boss planned to fire her the next day. Why was Ellison involved? He was having an affair with the young woman. He told the executive that if she were not performing as expected, then she should be terminated. See, the company came first.

I know you want to know what subsequently happened.

She was fired. Although they had been seeing each other for several months, she sued for sexual harassment, accusing Oracle and Ellison of termination for her decision to end the relationship. Oracle and Ellison came close to losing the case—after all, as Ellison even admitted, such action wasn't smart on the part of any CEO—but she lost her case when she manufactured evidence to prove her harassment charge against him.

As mentioned, Ellison isn't a paragon of virtue. But his personal lifestyle is no measure of his management ability. Oracle is the measure of that.

The results should be evident. Oracle is a fantastic company. Like many high-tech firms today, its stock value is being tested by a deepening economic downturn, as are sales by the capital market. However, if Oracle were to experience an economic downturn it couldn't have come at a better time for this company. Oracle has undergone major reinvention

> **Since its founding, Oracle has been more innovative, more efficient, and more directed when Ellison was actively involved in its management.**

and transformation that cut almost $1 billion from its expense line, an effort spearheaded by Ellison in his management/ leadership role as CEO.

As I look over the last twenty-five-plus years since Oracle was launched, I find that historically it has been more innovative, more efficient, and more directed when Ellison was actively involved in its management. Ellison played the lead role in the company's founding, steered it through its early years of rapid growth, and has grown fully into his management role since

1998, when he began transforming Oracle into a Web-based business (see Chapter 8). Many members of the press may think his role insubstantial in the years from Henley's and Lane's appearance (1990 to 1998), but Ellison's importance to the business was blurred by the Barnumesque role he played as spokesperson. Lane, as president, was the inside man, Ellison was the outside man and, as such, he took over a public relations role in addition to resuming the marketing role he had held in the early years of the company when his job was to sell the idea of relational databases.

Larry Ellison, Excellent Leader

Although ultimately Oracle's transformation to an e-business led to the resignation of Ray Lane, Ellison took a hands-on role in not only building an e-business from the former database software company, but also identifying and eliminating inefficiencies within the organization. How did Ellison manage it?

Management for Ellison is about centralized control—yes, with him in charge. He understands positive reinforcement, but if the carrot doesn't work, he'll go for the stick or negative reinforcement. For instance, when he initially asked Oracle's seventy country operations to work with him to consolidate information technology (IT) operations and databases at headquarters, they refused. He told them they could retain their own systems if they paid for them out of their own profits. Since profits are also the basis for bonuses, all country managers except the one for Canada agreed to consolidation. What happened with Canada? The subsidiary dragged its feet even after Ellison had sent an emissary— Gary Roberts, senior vice president of global information technology—to deliver an ultimatum. When that didn't work, Ellison shuffled management responsibilities. The problem disappeared.

By the end of 2000, the company had eliminated 2,000 server computers scattered around the world. All the company's data are now stored, as Ellison had wanted, on one central database accessible via the Web. This makes for easy accessibility—and not only for the worldwide organization. It makes it easier for Ellison to get a comprehensive view of operations and spot trouble before it gets out of hand. To quote Jeffrey O. Henley, the firm's chief financial officer, "Larry has the people in this company screwed down tight."[1]

Perhaps he overreacted to the inefficiencies he saw, but Ellison personally rewrote sales contracts and established standard pricing to cut down on dickering by the field sales force. He changed the compensation system to prevent more than one salesperson from getting a full commission on a sale. And he compensated country managers for meeting profit margin targets, not simply meeting sales goals at any cost.

In essence, Ellison has resumed a role he held prior to Lane's presidency, a role that with one major mishap—the 1990 near insolvency of Oracle—he had handled well. After the incident Ellison admitted that he could have been a better

CEO, more mindful of the numbers than he was. At a time when the workforce needed him to rally the troops, he was at home bandaging his ego for his failure to keep Oracle's growth on its previous upward path. The incident led to a decision that only a tough manager or leader could take. That was a recognition that he lacked the process skills that the company needed as it went through a major growth transition. Rather than contract with consultants who would leave never-read documents with him, he chose to bring on board professional managers to add balance to the entrepreneurial team he had assembled around him, executives like Jeff Henley and Ray Lane.

Although Ellison lacks an MBA in management, he clearly has the instincts of a business leader if you think back to the earlier policies he set and decisions he made for the fledgling Oracle. For one, he took the company international. This is unusual because the industry itself hadn't gone global in the early 1980s. Although Ellison had done no foreign travel, he saw the value that would come from moving Oracle into international markets. At first, the company worked with a distributor in Europe—Tom Peddersen Associates. It was 1984, and the money that came in from overseas sales was needed by the fledgling business. As soon as Oracle had a foothold in the European market, Ellison chose to buy out the distributor, converting all its employees to Oracle staff members. It was a pattern that Oracle used repeatedly to reach customers abroad.

Ellison and Oracle were ahead of other database software companies in adapting and selling products outside the United States. His company was the only one for some time that offered a global solution for multinational firms, enabling it to pursue the largest deals. Using distributors in the beginning was worthwhile because they offered immediate and efficient local support and a local sales presence without the expense of opening a satellite office or creating a subsidiary organization. Ultimately, however, Oracle set up its international operation of country managers. Equally valid as a leader when that international operation demanded tighter controls, he ensured that it happened.

BALANCING SALES AND PRODUCT DEVELOPMENT

During those early years, it was Ellison who, despite the role he carved for himself as top salesman, spoke up for balance between sales and product development. Even when the sales organization asked for new products or new versions with useless features to outsell the competition, Ellison stayed the course and was able to say no to members of the sales force and developers, even though it would have been easy for the company at that time to lose its focus—it often happens to entrepreneurial firms. Ellison knew that Oracle wasn't ready to expand to a second product line during those early years. Rather, he saw the worth of continuously updating the versions of the company's flagship product. Ellison created a strong development team under the direction of his partner

Bob Miner, and the two men focused research on advancing Oracle's core technology. Sanity prevailed in the development and release process, despite ongoing demands for new releases from the sales force. Miner became the organization's strong technical leader, but he had the backing of the strong CEO, Ellison. Consequently, the company could take advantage of the sales opportunities with which it was presented, but it would not allow itself to become so sales-centric that it lost a sense of its mission.

It was also Ellison who determined that the Oracle way to growth would not be by acquisition of technology or of other companies. Generally, young firms on a fast-growth path will opt to buy further growth by acquiring other's technology. Early on, Oracle experimented with a technology acquisition, purchasing a product it called Oracle SQL*Calc. On

> **Ellison determined that the Oracle path to growth would not be by acquisition.**

the surface, the technology seemed like a natural extension to Oracle's offerings, but it was not built the way other Oracle products were built. Consequently, it was difficult for Oracle developers to sustain the product and release new versions. Ultimately, the product disappeared from Oracle's line, as did the idea of buying growth. Oracle's CEO had learned that while it may take longer to develop technology internally, once it was complete you knew that it would fit well with the product line. Furthermore, there were no added purchasing costs.

There have, of course, been a few purchases of technology firms. There was even talk about Ellison purchasing Apple Computer, Inc. This proposed purchase was not to acquire technology; rather, it was prompted by the opportunity to gain Apple's industry experience and expand Oracle into new markets. Even this buy was passed on. At a time when the bigger companies have the choice to buy or make new business for themselves, Ellison and Oracle clearly come down on the "make" side of the issue.

Ellison as Visionary

At about the same time there was talk of buying Apple, Ellison told the industry at large about his company's network computing strategy at an industry conference. His announcement gave those most likely to be hurt by the network computer concept (or network appliance, as it is also called) the time to beat Oracle to the marketplace with a stronger sales appeal (see Chapter 7). Consequently, the network computer became a major lost opportunity for Oracle. Certainly, network computers would have given Oracle a second product line at a time when its flagship database line's marketplace was showing signs of eroding, but consumers weren't ready yet for Oracle to host their computer needs. After all, Microsoft was the major player in both the business *and* consumer markets.

Let's think further about the situation leading up to the network appliances Oracle was planning to develop. When Oracle had weathered the financial debacle of 1990, Ellison's role was more P. T. Barnum than CEO; he was pitchman for Oracle products as the outside man, and he saw a need for Oracle to grow beyond its limited business-to-business role—it needed to build awareness beyond IT if it was to regain lost growth from the 1990 situation. In 1993, he created Oracle's New Media division with the goal to develop database applications for multimedia data. In essence, the New Media division was formed to build database software to store audio, video, and graphics, as well as huge catalogs of text. Ellison's goal was to expand Oracle from simply a firm that managed numbers and information to an organization that managed information in any format. One of its breakthroughs was an Oracle database that could store digital video and deliver it to myriad users simultaneously.

Telephone companies heard about the development and wanted to offer video-on-demand to their customers; these telephone carriers were looking for a business that would make use of the bandwidth on their networks and allow them to expand their product offerings beyond simple voice calls. Ellison, the Oracle spokesman, touted the benefits of the new technology each and every time he could. He talked about enabling home shopping with a personal shopper, as well as home banking and all kinds of applications involving consumer interactivity. Ultimately, he talked about how consumers would no longer need a personal computer—they could use the television as their interface. Ellison, the corporate cheerleader, dubbed the project Alexandria, named for the world's first library in Alexandria, Egypt, to play up Oracle's role as a

> **Ellison's goal was to expand Oracle from simply a firm that managed numbers and information to an organization that managed information in any format.**

vast library as well, and talked up the project's "Excitement Factor." Oracle staff began wearing T-shirts with the New Media group's slogan: CHANGING THE WORLD.

Nothing became of Ellison's dream of interactive television. Indeed, nothing came of the subsequent network appliances, an idea that also initially came from the New Media operation but was embellished by Ellison. But both, in turn, led to a new vision of the role of Oracle as a service provider (see Chapter 10). Oracle's image significantly changed as a consequence of Ellison's public presentations of the idea of network computing—which may have had greater significance than the products that were being touted by Oracle. Ellison was seen as a visionary and his company was regarded as on the cutting edge.

The company's visibility grew. No longer were Oracle's products solely of interest to IT specialists. Suddenly chief information officers (CIOs), even CEOs, were interested in what Oracle was doing.

Leader/Visionary in the Software Industry

Larry Ellison is a leader in the software industry who's attuned to the needs of businesses. He's not only a CEO but a visionary CEO. While both Edward Oates and Bob Miner, Ellison's partners in founding Oracle, were interested in the relational database technology that came out of IBM Corp., keep in mind that it was Ellison who saw the commercial value in the technology—in a flash of insight. And, as important, he was also the individual who sold it to those within the corporate management community who had yet to see its value.

There were no promises, no guarantees that he would correctly anticipate the corporate customer's needs. Yet Ellison decided to take an extreme risk because he expected an immense return. He knew the market and understood some of the issues that businesses were facing based on his previous jobs, but for the most part it was a risk.

He also recognized the need to move ahead—to develop other software programs based on that flagship database to minimize the impact of a single failure. I was once told by a CEO whose organization had an impressive record for innovation that someone who had come up with three out of five successful ideas was ahead of the game—the best most people do is two out of five wins. Leaders of software companies recognize that failure isn't the exception—rather it is the rule. Consequently, they go for several wins to minimize the cost of failure.

They move quickly and they aim high—as Ellison did when he pushed Oracle's growth to 100 percent annually during its fledgling years. In his mind, getting big fast was a matter of survival. The software industry was moving quickly toward maturity, and Oracle had to be among the major players if it was to last.

If he were the kind of industry leader who could adapt quickly to trends, he also would have had to build a highly dynamic organization. Gates did it in 1995 when he stood before hundreds of analysts and reports and announced that he would refocus every project and every product to meet the Internet challenge. Ellison did it 1996 when he told, first, his own company and later the world press that his company saw the end of client/server computing and would reorganize to develop hosted applications software—and that it would save $1 billion by transforming its own internal operations via use of that software.

Ellison was also able to keep his promise because he had built Oracle into a flat, team-structured organization. The structure of an organization is a key leadership responsibility. The flatter, the more adaptable, the more suitable to move to meet the needs of client firms.

Take the values by which a business operates, add in the vigor of a strong management team, and the vision of someone who looks to the opportunities that change brings, and you will have an outstanding company. You will have Oracle and its oracle, Lawrence J. Ellison.

LOOKING
AHEAD

what's next for
Oracle and the
software industry?

Given his high profile, Larry Ellison has

become a brand unto his own, sometimes unintentionally taking attention away from his company, Oracle Corp. This is certainly what happened in summer 2000 when Ellison and his management team met with the press to discuss the company's development of a complete set of Internet-enabled business operations software and its own internal use of those products to save more than $1 billion annually. Instead, the press corps was interested in Ellison's plans for his new home and yacht *Sayonara*, his rivalry with Microsoft Corp., and his personal financial position.

Certainly, it must have been a frustrating time not only for Ellison's management team but Ellison himself, who had further business plans to share with the press yet found himself distracted by the nature of the other questions asked. It was only at the end of the meeting that Ellison was given the opportunity to play "the oracle of Oracle."

As he was leaving, a reporter asked him what he planned to do after he saved the company the $1 billion he promised. Ellison went so far as to promise that Oracle could probably achieve another billion dollars in savings after that, a promise he made again in 2001 while explaining how his firm was able to save the original $1 billion (or two-thirds of that amount, depending on how you figure the numbers). More important is what he said about the opportunity for revenue in the future.

Oracle would continue to develop and sell Internet-applicable software. The customer base for these products would grow as more and more companies gained an Internet presence. Then the oracle of Oracle went on to suggest that

> **Ellison suggests that the software industry as we know it now will vanish and be replaced by a service industry.**

the software industry as we know it now will vanish and be replaced by a service industry. This service industry will no longer require that companies buy their own computers, or hire their own staff to automate their business. They will buy automation systems on the Internet. Oracle's E-Business Suite will run on hosted computers at Oracle, "alleviating the headaches associated with managing software and hardware."[1]

This would have benefits both for customers and Oracle. For the customer, an Oracle-hosted application means a smaller upfront capital investment compared to a firm doing it on its own, because there would be no need to buy computer or network hardware, applications software, or server operating systems. Having the most up-to-date version of any application wouldn't be an issue for the customer because it would be the concern of the host—in other words, Oracle, which would guarantee the currentness of the product and would be responsible for broken components or upgrades of existing ones. Nor would the customer's information technology (IT) staff have to be knowledgeable about installing and administering either the hardware or software. Again, that would be Oracle's responsibility. Finally, at a time when talented IT personnel are expensive and in short supply, customers wouldn't need a support staff of application specialists.

Of course, Oracle would benefit. Hosting would represent a whole new business—albeit a service business—for the software developer. However, serving as host would enable Oracle to offer a customer more than it did before. Hosting a customer's site would also enable Oracle to become more closely integrated with the customer's business, thereby establishing a higher value proposition for a continued relationship with the customer (remember, "Lock the customer in, lock out the competition"). Oracle could then leverage all the expertise—maybe even costs in time—in product development when it creates the applications in the first place.

Knowledge learned in developing the application could also be used for installation, not to mention identification of problems for development of subsequent upgrades.

Oracle would use its own sales and support staffs to market the hosted applications, so there would be no need for additional staff in either areas. Maybe best of all, Oracle could choose what other software would run on the servers that it hosted—which would mean no Microsoft or IBM best-of-breed packaged software.

The concept makes sense for any software company, not only Oracle, as Ray Lane, formerly president at Oracle and now a principal at one of the top venture capitalist firms, noted. According to Lane, the software industry's Net-based business model in which applications from various vendors are forced together only creates integration problems. Making upgrades work only means further troubles and adds to customer costs. Since applications have to be sold by sales forces or other distribution channels, companies pay more than a half dollar for each dollar made, whereas sales and downloads directly from the Internet would be less than R&D costs—about 15 cents per dollar. And, of course, through digital delivery, software developers would activate new application features on customers' services rather than demand customers replace old versions with new ones across multiple IT systems, according to Lane. In Lane's view, "virtual" is the best route for all software firms just as it is for many businesses.[2]

That was the future that Ellison envisioned in 2000. Businesses would run their shop floor, retail outlet, or chain of restaurants using the Oracle E-Business Suite off the Internet. They would turn to Oracle as the applications software provider to host their enterprise resource planning (ERP) and customer relationship management (CRM) software needs and any other software needs. "Oracle would be the service provider," according to Ellison, "because it offers the whole stack."[3] The fact that Oracle offered a complete suite of programs would keep Oracle in its number-one position, in his opinion. As is his practice in spinning off subsidiary companies, Ellison named Oracle's service firm Oracle Business OnLine.

At the same time, Ellison talked about his company developing and spinning off a large number of subsidiary companies, though Oracle would retain part ownership, a majority interest, or full control of each. For example, there is OracleMobile, for wireless technology and RetailersMarket Xchange.com that supports Amazon.com.

I would assume that somewhere in Ellison's mind may also be thoughts about network computing. Although Oracle's first efforts with the idea failed, the failure was in execution, not in the strategic idea. Clearly, customers would be interested in less expensive ways to access Oracle databases. Ellison has set up an operation to look into wireless technology, which may give birth to a PalmPilot–type setup with no bit of Microsoft software. After all, the PalmPilot offers everything that the network computer was to have—it is small, light, user-friendly, and offers only a handful of applications.

We can expect new database software developments in global commerce, electronic communication, real-time processing, maintenance of virtual inventories, warehousing for companies that do not maintain inventory (like the original

> Oracle's first efforts with network computing failed, but the failure was in execution, not in the strategic idea.

Amazon model), and available-to-promise systems (like Levis order entry system) and configure-to-order ordering systems—all business trends anticipated by Ellison and his management team.

All of this makes a lot of sense in high-techdom, but what has been the response to date in the marketplace?

As of mid-June 2001, applications sales were extremely disappointing, according to research analyst Mark Verbeck with Epoch Partners. The gap may be due, in part, to the economy, as Oracle's chief financial officer, Jeffrey O. Henley, has noted. However, it may also be due to the fact that there are many companies—upstarts and major players—jumping into the application service provider (ASP) marketplace. Among the major players are three long-time Oracle adversaries: SAP AG, IBM Corp., and yes, Microsoft. After all, the software applications market represents $74 billion. Only one percent of companies rent software through ASPs, but that market, too, is expected to grow—to $11.3 billion by the year 2006.

The Other Players

IBM is backing a best-of-breed approach to the market, partnering with major application makers such as SAP, Siebel Systems, Inc., and PeopleSoft, Inc., not to mention many upstarts. These firms see a need to partner since a dominate Oracle will mean little market room for themselves. IBM needs these partners, too, since it doesn't sell applications on its own. Still, because it was in the game ahead of Oracle, IBM already is ahead, with 30 percent market share (or three times Oracle's share), according to Giga Information Group.

German software giant SAP had chosen to sell both applications software and hosting services. But the latter offering failed miserably in the market as it tried to strong-arm customers into choosing only SAP applications. Now client firms are encouraged to choose between SAP products and software sold by others, a move that has enabled the company to grow 29 percent compared to a 3 percent decline for Oracle—which continues to sell its package of Oracle applications.

As for Microsoft, it could be seen as a crouching tiger ready to spring forth with a plan that ties together just about every Microsoft product, from back-end office to front-end client applications, from cell phone software to server software—all across the Internet. Called simply or aptly Microsoft.Net, the strategy would allow individuals or companies to rent any

Internet-based service from Microsoft or one of its allies. Already Microsoft is making inroads in the server software that runs Web sites, an area that Oracle and Sun Microsystems, Inc. have dominated.

Oracle's Answer

Oracle sees an exciting future, but one in which there will be intense competition. There are too many start-ups making too many promises. Add in the current uncertain economic situation, including the downfall of the dot-coms, which made a Web presence less popular even in legacy firms, and the tightening capital market, and it is understandable why the numbers at Oracle haven't yet met the company's expectations. Given the costs in dollars and time, customers that have already invested in existing applications are reluctant to dismantle and replace them with Oracle applications. For many firms, bringing in Oracle to host their Web operation would require a major strategic shift— and a political one—to occur.

Prior to September 11, 2001, Oracle saw an economic turnaround by the end of 2001. According to Jeremy Burton, an Oracle senior vice president, initial efforts at hosting involved ASPs purchasing packages from software publishers and implementing them piecemeal. This made for poor quality for customers and large expense for the hosts. According to Burton, Oracle learned early the value of standardized configurations and standardized versions of applications to keep costs down and launches more readily deliverable. "We rearchitectured some of our applications to make them the kind born for hosting, and these new born-of-hosting applications can support multiple companies in a single instance," he has said.[4]

So the oracle of Oracle and his management team would seem to believe that there will be greater outsourcing in the future, and Oracle will significantly benefit despite initial weak market results. What else?

The company's own move onto the Web and subsequent e-business transformation suggests the next trend. That is, Oracle sees a move toward intercompany integration. I'm not talking solely about tying corporate systems together. That

> **Oracle sees an exciting future, but one in which there will be intense competition.**

has already been done, and if not at your firm, you are advised to read about the benefits of relational databases. But here I am talking about increasing numbers of companies emulating the Dell Computer model; that is, integrating their own business systems with those of other companies, especially suppliers and customers. Oracle has done it, and its E-Business Suite is designed to enable other companies to emulate it.

Finally, as e-business applications from Oracle suggest, Oracle's CEO sees a major trend toward automated processes and trade—that is, there'll be less need for people as computers handle the transactions and paper processing they previously did.

There are obstacles to the future for Oracle as envisioned by Ellison. For one, the economy is more uncertain than it was in mid-2001. While companies seem more likely to cut marketing and training dollars than IT investments, the deepness

> **The next trend: a move toward intercompany integration.**

of any economic downturn will determine how much companies are willing to invest in data management, let alone a more substantive Web presence. Keep in mind that the initial idea behind Oracle's investment in applications software was the ever-increasing numbers of new dot-coms on the Web. There were projections that we would see a whole new group of dot-coms before 2001 was out. From chips to wireless to information technology, an article in *Forbes* entitled "Internet II: Rebooting America," projected that the biggest economic boom in history was bearing down on the United States. That boom would include sleeker, smarter, more agile dot-coms, eclipsing the Web boom from 1992 to 1999. But that projection came out one day before terrorist attacks in New York, Virginia, and Pennsylvania on September 11, 2001.

Even before that second day that will live in infamy, there were those who worried about the use of the R-word (recession) in the news. Certainly, after the dot-com downfall in the late 1990s, venture capitalists, while unlikely to turn away a potential eBay or Amazon.com, certainly will be giving greater scrutiny to any plans for Web-based businesses, especially retail firms.

There may be questions, too, raised in corporate board rooms about the benefits of some Web-based applications, CRM in particular. A white paper by Mercer Management Consulting released in fall 2001 reported results of a study by Data Warehousing Institute in March 2001 that found that only 16 percent of the companies that had implemented CRM software believed it had exceeded their expectations. On the other hand, 41 percent considered the effort "a potential flop," quoting the Mercer white paper.

Another Mercer white paper, "The xSP Revolution, Round 2," issued in Fall 2001, again issued prior to the terrorist attacks on the United States, spoke about "a big wave of adoption and revenue growth" ahead, but it also observed that the demand will be for applications customers want, not the latest cool technology. Which could help Oracle—which is known for its customer-centric attitude—but also has built its reputation on offering the "newest" or "cutting-edge" technology. The white paper gives Oracle Business Online high points as an integrated suite provider, but it observes that customer adoption for it will be slow, impeded by the high cost of switching from current "good enough" software systems and vendors.

The Mercer white paper is in agreement with Ellison's software as a service model, but it suggests that software companies too often focus on rewriting code and give little attention to their customers' total economic systems and how their offerings can assist. The white paper concludes by suggesting that the winner in the applications marketplace will be that organization with a business design that reflects the myriad corporate concerns as businesses migrate to the latest applications.

For the software industry in general, and Oracle in particular, there will be challenges ahead—but opportunities, too.

So, as we end this book, we are left with many unanswered questions about the future economy and Oracle's place in it. And our biggest question, What is Larry Ellison really like? I believe he's the new millennium's Barnum, a larger-than-life billionaire who enjoys the kind of life we all think we would want. He's a man who early in his career sometimes humbugged his customers with half-truths and empty promises but also built one of the largest software companies from scratch with a single idea, and in the public's eye continues to create the "world's greatest show" because he has learned that it will get your attention—which also means that Oracle will get your attention.

There is very little difference between the Oracle with a capital *O* and the oracle with a lowercase *o*—you see, they are so interlinked that the man is the company, and the company is the product of a lifetime of proving to the world just how successful that man could be.

appendix
timeline of events at oracle

AUGUST 17, 1944 Lawrence Joseph Ellison is born in New York City to his unwed mother. After he recovers from a serious bout of pneumonia, he is given to his aunt and uncle to raise in Chicago.

1966 After making a second effort to graduate from college, he drops out of the University of Chicago and relocates to California, where he works as a programmer.

1967 Ellison marries Adda Quinn. A graduate of San Jose University studying secondary education at Berkeley, she thinks he is the most fascinating man she had ever met. They divorce in 1973.

1975 Larry Ellison meets Edward Oates and Robert Miner, the two career programmers who were to become his early partners in Oracle. In those years, Miner was to become known as "the steak" and Ellison "the sizzle."

1976 Ellison marries his second wife, Nancy Wheeler. She's from an "aristocratic family" in Louisville, Kentucky.

1977 Ellison partners with Miner and Oates in forming Software Development Laboratories (SDL).

1977 Ellison divorces Wheeler. Because they had married in California and he had been head of SDL during that time, she was entitled to half his shares in SDL under the state's community property statute. Since the company has yet to show any success, she settles for $500.

1978 SDL relocates and changes its name to Relational Software Inc., to reflect the relational database management (RDBMS) product it is developing. Consulting work keeps the company afloat until it begins to sell versions of the Oracle RDBMS.

1980 Oates, with marital problems, sells his shares back to the company—the value estimated then, is $20,000. Oates receives $10,000 in cash, which he gives to his wife as part of divorce proceedings, and a promissory note for another $10,000 from the company. Ellison also loans Oates $40,000 to purchase a house.

1982 There is another name change. The company takes on the name of its only product. Oracle Corp. is born.

1983 Ellison marries Barbara Boothe, whom he met when she applied for the position of receptionist. Their courtship begins via e-mail. Minutes before the wedding, he presents her with a prenuptial agreement for her signature. She signs it but when they divorce years later the courts put aside the prenuptial agreement because of the conditions under which it was signed.

1986 Oracle goes public at $15 a share, earning Ellison $90 million in a single day.

1990 Oracle experiences financial crisis stemming from a decision to decentralize financial management. Costs Ellison in excess of $350 million. Oracle stock plummets.

1991 Ellison makes the tough decision to bring in experienced business professionals to help manage fast-growing Oracle. The first hire is Jeff Henley as CFO.

1992 Ray Lane comes on board as vice-president of sales and over time recruits and trains corps of professional managers.

1995 Ellison takes first steps to create a second product line, promoting the concept of network appliances and interactive TV. Oracle's CEO predicts the demise of the PC.

1996 Ellison appoints Ray Lane president. Lane assumes control inside as Ellison becomes the voice of Oracle to the press and client base, providing advance notice of new software versions and product opportunities.

1997 Ellison's vision of network appliances reaches the marketplace too late. Rival Bill Gates of Microsoft Corp. improves administration of Microsoft products and helps drive down the costs of PCs. Rather than depose the PC, the network appliance concept spurs the market for inexpensive PCs.

1998 Ellison sees opportunity in the Internet as a delivery platform for applications software; decrees that development efforts focus exclusively there—no more clientserver applications.

1999 Ellison is disappointed at initial efforts, but remains determined to spearhead process. He identifies inefficiencies within his company and the benefits of transforming Oracle into an e-business.

2000 Ellison resumes responsibilities of president, making Lane's role unnecessary. Lane resigns. Shortly thereafter, Gary Bloom, thought to be a serious internal candidate for top post, resigns to head up Veritas Software Corp., as it becomes evident that Ellison has taken complete charge at Oracle.

2001 Release of Oracle's first Internet applications prompts complaints. Competition grows in the marketplace—from Microsoft, IBM, SAP, and Hewlett-Packard. A weak economy and the dot-com shakeout raise further questions about Oracle's strategy.

notes

CHAPTER 1

1. Wilson, Mike. *The Difference Between God and Larry Ellison: Inside Oracle Corporation* (New York: William Morrow, 1997).

2. *Ibid.*, p. 58.

3. Kaplan, David A. *The Silicon Boys and Their Valley of Dreams* (New York: Perennial, Harper/Collins Publishers, Inc., 1999), p. 40; and Wilson, Mike. *The Difference Between God and Larry Ellison*, *op. cit.*, p. 130.

4. Server, Andy, "The Next Richest Man in the World." *Fortune*, November 13, 2000.

5. Wilson, Mike. *op. cit.*, p. 60.

6. Kaplan, David A. *op. cit.*, p. 140.

7. Wilson, Mike. *op. cit.*, p. 74.

8. Kaplan, David A. *op. cit.*, p. 138.

9. Wilson, Mike. *op. cit.*, p. 91.

10. *Ibid*, p. 103.

11. *Ibid*, p. 88.

12. Kaplan, David A. *op. cit.*, p. 140.

13. Frei, Frances, "Oracle Corporation," *Inside Business and Consumer Software*, Harvard Business School Publishing, HBSP Number 4894, copyright 2001, p. 27.

14. Wilson, Mike. *op. cit.*, p. 254

15. Frei, Frances, *op. cit.*, p. 29.

16. Server, Andy, *op. cit.*

CHAPTER 2

1. Sinton, Peter, "The Villa That Oracle Built," *SF Gate Morning Fix*, April 21, 2001.

2. Wilson, Mike. *The Difference Between God and Larry Ellison: Inside Oracle Corporation* (New York: William Morrow, 1997).

3. *Ibid*, p. 184.

4. Kaplan, David A. *The Silicon Boys and Their Valley of Dreams* (New York: Perennial, Harper/Collins Publishers, Inc., 1999), p. 123.

5. Murray, Dan, "Larry Ellison, Crusader"

CHAPTER 3

1. Hawn, Carleen, "The Trouble with Larry," *Forbes*, August 20, 2001.

2. Read, Stuart. *The Oracle Edge* (Holbrook, Massachusetts: Adams Media Corporation, 2000).

3. *Ibid*, p. 12.

4. *Ibid*, p. 12.

5. *Ibid*, p. 171.

6. *Ibid*, p. 172.

7. Kaplan, David A. *The Silicon Boys and Their Valley of Dreams* (New York: Perennial, Harper/Collins Publishers, Inc., 1999), p. 140.

8. Server, Andy, "The Next Richest Man in the World," *Fortune*, November 13, 2000.

9. Remark from Oracle sales representative to author.

10. Hawn, Carleen. "The Trouble with Larry," *Forbes*, August 20, 2001.

11. *Ibid.*

CHAPTER 4

1. Kaplan, David A. *The Silicon Boys and Their Valley of Dreams* (New York: Perennial, Harper/Collins Publishers, Inc., 1999), p. 18.

2. Schlender, Brent, "Larry Ellison: Oracle at Web Speed, *Fortune*, May 24, 1999.

3. Read, Stuart. *The Oracle Edge* (Holbrook, Massachusetts: Adams Media Corporation, 2000), p. 6.

4. *Ibid*, p. 125.

5. Kaplan, David A. *op. cit.*, p. 256.

6. *Ibid*, p. 150.

7. *Ibid*, p. 142.

8. LaMonica, Paul, "Loving Larry," *Red Herring*, November 27, 2000.

9. Kaplan, David A. *op. cit.*, p. 149.

10. Press release from IBM.

CHAPTER 5

1. Read, Stuart. *The Oracle Edge* (Holbrook, Massachusetts: Adams Media Corporation, 2000), p. 86.

2. Interview with Bruce Alper, CIO for AMA.

3. E-Commerce Software, *Industry Standard*, June 4, 2000.

4. *Ibid*.

CHAPTER 6

1. The Standish Group *(www.standishgroup.com)*.

2. Behnam Tabrizi and Rick Walleigh, "Defining Next-Generation Products," *Harvard Business Review*, (November–December 1997).

3. Frei, Frances, "Oracle Corporation," *Inside Business and Consumer Software*, Harvard Business School Publishing, HBSP Number 4894, copyright 2001, p. 27.

CHAPTER 7

1. Flamholtz, Eric, *Growing Pains: Transitioning from an Entrepreneurship to a Professionally Managed Firm.* Management Systems Consulting Corp. (San Francisco: Jossey-Bass, 2000), p. 29.

2. Wilson, Mike. *The Difference Between God and Larry Ellison: Inside Oracle Corporation* (New York: William Morrow, 1997), p. 216.

3. Kaplan, David, *op. cit.*, p. 145.

4. Consol, Mike, "The Grand Obsessions of Larry Ellison," *San Francisco Business Times*, (January 13, 1997).

5. Corcoran, Elizabeth, "Oracle: Walking the Talk," *Forbes*, (August 2001).

CHAPTER 8

1. Hawn, Carleen, "The Trouble with Larry," *Forbes*, August 20, 2001.

2. Schlender, Brent, "Larry Ellison: Oracle at Web Speed," *Fortune*, May 24, 1999.

3. *Ibid.*

4. Hawn, Carleen, *op. cit.*

5. Lewis, Bob, "IS Survival Guide: Are Mr. Ellison's Vanilla Flavor-Style Customer Relations Good for You?" *InfoWorld*, April 2, 2001.

6. Schlender, Brent, *op. cit.*

7. Barrenechea, Mark J. *E-Business or Out of Business: Oracle's Roadmap for Profiting in the New Economy* (New York: McGraw-Hill, 2001), p. 5.

8. *Ibid.*, p. 7.

9. Hawn, Carleen, *op. cit.*

10. Interview with author.

CHAPTER 9

1. "The CFO's Perspective: An Interview with Jeffrey O. Henley, CFO, Oracle Corporation," *Financial Executive*, May-June 1999.

CHAPTER 10

1. Frei, Frances, "Oracle Corporation," *Inside Business and Consumer Software*, Harvard Business School Publishing, HBSP Number 4894, copyright 2001, p. 25.

2. Schlender, Brent, "Oracle at Web Speed," Fortune, May 24, 1999.

3. Frei, Frances, *op. cit.*, p. 26.

4. *Ibid*, p. 27.

bibliography

BOOKS

Anonymous. *The Company Insider: Oracle.* San Francisco: The Wet Feet Press, 1998.

Barrenechea, Mark. *E-Business or Out of Business: Oracle's Roadmap for Profiting in the New Economy.* New York: McGraw-Hill, 2001.

Dell, Michael with Catherine Fredman. *Direct from Dell: Strategies That Revolutionized an Industry.* New York: HarperCollins Publishers, Inc., 2000.

Flamholtz, Eric. *Growing Pains: Transitioning from an Entrepreneurship to a Professionally Managed Firm. Management Systems Consulting Corp.*, San Francisco: Jossey-Bass, 2000.

Hock, Detlev J., et al. *Secrets of Software Success: Management Insights from 100 Software Firms Around the World.* New York: McKinsey & Co., 2000.

Kaplan, David A. *The Silicon Boys and Their Valley of Dreams.* New York: Perennial, Harper/Collins Publishers, Inc., 1999.

Read, Stuart. *The Oracle Edge: How Oracle Corporation's Take No Prisoners Strategy Has Made an $8 Billion Software Powerhouse.* Holbrook, MA: Adams Media Corporation, 2000.

Sigismund, Charles G. *Champions of Silicon Valley: Visionary Thinking from Today's Technology Pioneers.* New York: John Wiley & Sons, 2000.

Wilson, Mike. *The Difference Between God and Larry Ellison: Inside Oracle Corporation.* New York: William Morrow & Co., 1997.

ARTICLES

Adshead, Antony. "Big Three Battle Over Slowing Database Market," *Computer Weekly*, June 7, 2001.

Anonymous. "E-Commerce Software," *Industry Standard*, June 4, 2001.

———. "Emerging Technology: .Net Gain?" *CIO Magazine*, July 2, 2001.

———. "Gartner Dataquest Says Worldwide Database Software Market Grew 10%," *EDP Weekly's IT Monitor*, June 4, 2001.

———. "IBM vs. Oracle: It Could Get Bloody," *BusinessWeek Online*, May 28, 2001.

———. "1.5 Million Developers Register on Oracle Technology Network," *Online Product News*, July 2001.

———. "Oracle Sees Business Booming," *South China Morning Post*, March 27, 2001.

———. "Oracle: Why It's Cool Again," *BusinessWeek Online*, May 8, 2000

———. "Software: Hard to Overlook," *BusinessWeek Online*, October 26, 2000.

———. "Tales We've Heard (and Told) About the PCs Successors," *CIO Magazine*, June 1, 2001.

———. "The CFO's Perspective: An Interview with Jeffrey O. Henley, CFO, Oracle Corporation," *Financial Executive*, May–June 1999.

———. "Who Will Help Run Oracle? Ask Again Later," *Business Week*, December 4, 2000.

Baker, Stephen. "Hasso Plattner on SAP's Web-Wise Makeover," *BusinessWeek Online*, May 5, 1999.

Consol, Mike. "The Grand Obsessions of Larry Ellison," *San Francisco Business Times*, January 13, 1997.

Corcoran, Elizabeth. "Oracle: Walking the Talk," *Forbes*, August 2001.

Dembreck, Chet. "Oracle, Chevron, Wal-Mart Unit Form B2B Exchange," *E-Commerce Times*, March 9, 2000.

Donahue, Sean. "The Real Billon-Dollar Man," *Business 2.0*, www.business2.com/articles/mag/print/0,1643,14444,00. html.

Doyle, Eric. "Oracle Fast-Forwards Mobile E-Mail," *Computer Weekly*, May 24, 2001.

Ellison, Larry. "How We Saved a Billion Dollars," *White Paper*, Oracle Corporation, 2000.

Frei, Frances. "Oracle Corporation," *Inside Business and Consumer Software*, Harvard Business School Publishing, HBSP Number 4894, copyright 2001.

Harvey, Phil. "Larry Ellison Pushes Another Non-PC Biz Plan," *Red Herring Magazine*, , February 23, 2000.

Hatlestad, Luc. "Speaking to the Future," *Red Herring Magazine*, August 1, 1997.

Hill, G. Christian. "Dog Eats Dog Food, and Damn If It Ain't Tasty," *e-Business*, November 2000.

Jacobs, Ken. "ISVs as ASPs," *Oracle Magazine*, July-August 2001.

Jones, Jennifer. "Oracle, Sun Dial e911 Apps," *InfoWorld*, June 11, 2001.

LaMonica, Paul R. "Loving Larry," *Red Herring Communications*, November 27, 2000.

Lashinsky, Adam. "How Ranting, Raving Larry Ellison Has Come to Look Like a Visionary," *TheStreet.com*, November 17, 1999.

Lee, Katherine. "CEO Larry Ellison's Accurate Oracle," *HR.com*, August 3, 2001.

Lewis, Bob. "Survival Guide: The ERP, CRM Difference," *InfoWorld*, May 21, 2001.

————. "IS Survival Guide: Are Mr. Ellison's Vanilla Flavor-Style Customer Relations Good for You?" *InfoWorld*, April 2, 2001.

Lipson, Steve. "A Giant Leap in E-Business Database Evolution," *Oracle Magazine*, July-August 2001.

Malone, Michael. "Internet II: Rebooting America," *Forbes*, September 10, 2001.

Mandel, Michael and Robert D. Hof. "Rethinking the Internet," *The Standard*, March 26, 2001.

Mathewson, James. "Oracle: A Bargain," *Computer.com*, January 2001.

McKinsey, Kitt. "Interview: Larry Ellison: New Landscape," *Far Eastern Economic Review*, April 5, 2001.

Murray, Dan. "Larry Ellison, Crusader," *www.livingstonmontana.com/access/dan/214larry ellisoncrusader.html.*

Olofson, Carl W. "Oracle Internet File System: Providing Comprehensive Management of e-Business Information," IDC White Paper (Framingham, MA: International Data Corp., 2000.

Powell, Bonnie Azab. "Mission Impossible?" *Red Herring Magazine*, August 1, 2000.

Richtel, Matt. "Mixed Report from Oracle," *New York Times*, June 19, 2001.

Schlender, Brent. "Larry Ellison: Oracle at Web Speed," *Fortune*, May 24, 1999.

——. Oracle at Web Speed: The Internet Changes Everything and the CEO of Oracle Is Living Proof," *eCompany*, May 1999.

Server, Andy. "The Next Richest Man in the World," *Fortune*, November 13, 2000.

SIIA. "Information Companies Face Immediate Online Challenges," July 19, 2000, *www.trendsreport.net/release2.html.*

Sinton, Peter. "The Villa That Oracle Built," SF *Gate Morning Fix*, April 21, 2001.

Slywotsky, Adrian. "Digital Edge: Four Lessons from Larry," *Fortune*, March 5, 2001.

Stone, Amey. "Microsoft, Through Long-Term Lenses," *BusinessWeek Online*, February 22, 2001.

——. "Keeping Legacy Software Alive," *BusinessWeek Online*, June 14, 2001.

Tabrizi, Behnam and Rick Walleigh. "Defining Next-Generation Products," *Harvard Business Review*, November–December 1997.

Verton, Dan. "Oracle Hit Again by Top-Level Resignation," *ComputerWorld*, November 27, 2000.

Ward-Button, Neil. "The Big Boys Learn to Play Together," *Computer Weekly*, May 10, 2001.

index